Creative Drama:
Enhancing Self-Concepts and Learning

by

Sue Renard
and
Kay Sockol

Publisher—

EDUCATIONAL MEDIA CORPORATION®
P.O. Box 21311
Minneapolis, MN 55421

Production editor—

Don L. Sorenson

Graphic design—

Earl Sorenson

Artwork—

Michael Craig

Dedication

To our parents...

Juanita and Harold Lyon
Fan and Ovid Walls

...who, from the very beginning, gave us an
incredible sense of belonging, uniqueness and personal power.
They helped us to believe in ourselves and to know
that we could make a difference in the lives of others.

Table of Contents

About the Authors

Sue Renard and Kay Sockol are elementary counselors with tenacious beliefs in the potential for growth, despite age or personal circumstances, as a result of experiencing creative drama activities in this book! They conduct workshops and seminars on the use of creative drama, self-esteem and personal growth, management techniques, communication and parenting skills.

The authors have been active in education for twenty years, working with children from nursery school through adolescence. More recently they have become interested in using creative drama in geriatric settings.

Sue Lyon Renard holds a B.S. degree from Purdue University in Home Economics and a M.Ed. in Counseling and Human Psychology form Texas Women's University. She is a National Certified Counselor and a Licensed Professional Counselor in the State of Texas. She is married to a professional engineer and is the mother of three grown children.

Kay Walls Sockol received a B.S. degree in Elementary Education from The University of Texas at Austin and a M.Ed. in Guidance and Counseling from Hardin-Simmons University. She is a National Certified Counselor and a Consultant with the Creative Drama Network of Texas. She is married to an accountant and is the mother of a teen-age daughter.

Introduction

Creative Drama—
A Motivating Force

Tell me and I forget.
Show me and I remember.
Involve me and I understand.

The concept of self has been demonstrated to be highly influential in much of an individual's behavior and to be directly related to one's general personality and state of well-being. To develop self-esteem, children need to feel recognized and approved by other members of their group. We have found that participation in creative drama is an effective method of enhancing self-esteem. It is also a strong motivating technique for learning. Creative drama personalizes the learning process by integrating experience with thoughts and feelings.

Concentration, sensory and emotional awareness, communication, movement, imagination and cooperation are key processes incorporated in creative drama. Creative drama is process-oriented, non-scripted and spontaneous. The facilitator encourages participants or "players" to imagine, enact and reflect upon a variety of human experiences. All players have opportunities to become active in a non-judgmental environment. Though creative drama is spontaneous, it is not haphazard. To the contrary, the facilitator leads participants in systematic, organized activity which has a specific focus or objective.

As a guidance and teaching tool, creative drama promotes thinking, learning and social skills in a variety of ways as it:
- [ ] increases ability to communicate thoughts and feelings.
- [ ] develops concentration, attentive listening, observational and discussion skills.
- [ ] fosters spontaneity, imagination and visualization.
- [ ] encourages growth of originality, flexibility and elaboration of thinking.
- [ ] creates an environment for feeling successful.
- [ ] sharpens the dynamics of group process in cooperation, planning, decision-making and evaluating.
- [ ] is just plain fun!

Creative drama is the vehicle we use to help children experience the five aspects of emotional well-being necessary for the development and maintenance of a healthy self-concept.

Through years of experience, we have refined the materials presented in this book to enable children to engage in creative drama activities to enhance their senses of belonging, power, uniqueness, and to understand more about models and processes. As an aid to remembering the concepts, we refer to this as the B-PUMP model.

Belonging
Children with a sense of belonging feel content and at peace with themselves. Belonging occurs when children perceive that they have a part in a relationship that is important to them and to others. Belonging also occurs when children feel that objects, body functions, senses, thoughts and emotions are their own. The more children feel that they belong, the more free they are to take the risk of trying new experiences, thus discovering more about themselves.

Power
Children with a healthy sense of power feel that they can make choices for themselves that are both beneficial to them and acceptable to others in their environment. They are confident of their ability to see the appropriate thing to do under different circumstances and they are able to act on their decisions. They know when to deal directly with a situation and when to ask for help. They can determine alternative methods for dealing with their emotions, making decisions and solving problems.

Uniqueness
Children with a sense of uniqueness feel that they have qualities and strengths that set them apart from other people and that make them special. The more they understand their special attributes, the more they are able to contribute to family, friends and society.

Models
Children with positive role models have behaviors which resemble those of people they admire, trust and love. As children grow, they adopt certain behavior patterns and reject others. Children with positive models demonstrate behavioral qualities that are beneficial to themselves and others.

Process
Children who know the "how to's" in accomplishing tasks feel capable of mastering new experiences. They can try activities with a degree of success because they understand processes. They are willing to be taught processes for decision making and problem solving that will aid them in accomplishing life tasks.

How to Use This Book

The activities presented have been designed to enhance the following components of a healthy self-concept: sense of belonging, sense of power, and sense of uniqueness. Self-esteem is also increased when lessons focus on the importance of role models in deciding on personal behavior. Self-worth is elevated by the security of knowing how to go about doing a task, or how a process happens.

Chapters I through III are developmental and sequential because they are building blocks for techniques used in creative drama. Chapter I, "Beginning Lessons," gives plans which establish group cohesion, teaches skills needed for future lessons, and gives facilitators techniques for implementing activities. Chapter II, "Playing Skills," provides activities to teach the skills of concentration, sensory and emotional awareness, movement, imagination, communication and cooperation.

Chapter III, "Playmaking Skills," includes instruction in the development of characterization, dialogue, plot, theme or idea. Facilitators are encouraged to use these first lessons to become familiar with the basic elements in the creative drama process. The progression of lessons is most effective when an entire class is involved simultaneously in the guided activity before working in pairs, and then interacting in small groups.

Chapters IV through VIII need not be used sequentially. Each lesson within a chapter stands alone and can be presented as the facilitator desires or wishes to emphasize one of the five components of healthy self-esteem.

Each lesson follows this format:

Focus:
What are key concepts in this activity? Key words come from learning objectives in subjects taught and from guidance curricula.

Introduction:
What is the guidance rationale for this activity? How will key concepts be helpful in enhancing self-esteem and learning?

Preparation:
How can participants be prepared to go into the main drama lesson? What psychomotor activity and sensory motivation will be effective? Included here are "Warm-ups" and "Cool-downs," short activities designed to introduce or conclude the directed activities.

Warm-ups and Cool-downs. A warm-up activity is short, easily performed, and involves all of the class to prepare them for creative drama activity. Effectiveness is in clear, concise directions and modeling given by the adult leader. An open area is desirable, so that persons have enough "playing space" to swing their arms and legs without touching others. A circle formation often is advantageous; however, children may stand behind their desks for warm-ups and cool-downs.

From the guidance perspective, there is a need for closure at the end of a lesson. The psychological affect of true learning often intensifies body action and emotion. Children are usually excited during creative drama. The ending and transition is vitally important to help children channel their enthusiasm.

A "cool-down" activity aids the children in calming down physiologically and emotionally after the lesson. This is important in helping both facilitator and students in experiencing a pleasant transition from the drama activity to the next class. Each lesson in this book has a suggested "warm-up" and a "cool-down."

Directions and Activities:
How will the activity or "problem" be structured? What organizational process needs to be explained? What rules are needed? Which grouping methods are best suited to work on the problem: individual, in unison as a class, in pairs or in small groups?

Discussion:
What kinds of questions will enable participants to engage in the high level thought processes of knowledge application, analysis and synthesis? The discussion at the end of each lesson is important to the proper conclusion of the creative drama activity. It is through the discussion and sharing time that "aha's"—flashes of insight—happen and information is integrated and assimilated.

Summary:
What are the main objectives of the creative drama activity? These statements are for the facilitator's convenience in reviewing the key concepts with the participants.

Invitation to Facilitators

We invite you to join us in the motivational experience of exploring and understanding more about human growth through the energizing process of creative drama.

Our aim is to help you develop new understanding about building and maintaining self-worth, and add the creative drama technique to your facilitative repertoire. As you, the reader, become more familiar with the creative drama concept, we hope that your own unique ideas for using this technique will emerge. For facilitators, as well as participants, we wish you the joy of sharing fun and laughter—ingredients which add to richness in daily living!

Chapter I
Begining Lessons

Be an Animal, Lesson 1.2
Be an Inanimate Object, Lesson 1.3

Making Our Rules for Creative Drama

Grades: K-8

Focus:

Players, audience, pantomime, personal space, respect, sensory and emotional recall

Introduction:

When children understand the reason and need for rules, they are more likely to follow them. In experiencing a step-by-step development of simple rules, they are cooperatively building a framework for proper interactions. Planning with the facilitator creates a high sense of personal regard and worth.

Preparation: Ocean Waves

Warm-up. *"Reach out with your arms as far as you can.... Pretend you are the ocean waves splashing back and forth; add sounds."*

Cool-down. *"Now, become a lake.... Have calm movements... and now sit down."*

Directed Activity 1:

Direct the children to stand in a circle and show with their bodies that they are happy... and ready to listen. *"What is the difference in the way we acted?"* (When showing "happy" there is laughter, some movement; when showing "ready to listen" bodies are calm, faces are turned to the teacher expectantly.)

"In our creative drama time, we will be doing things that involve much more moving and talking than in a class for language arts or math. Let us think of important things to remember that will help everyone to get along."

Direct a group of six to be "players" for the following activity, while others are "audience" members. One student is chosen to be the director. Give directions to the others for acting out a story about a family of three bears who are having a party for their friends, the rabbit and the robin.

Discussion:

1. *"What was important for you to do to understand directions?"* (Listen, do not talk all at once, etc.)

2. *"If a character does not understand what to do, how could that person show confusion?"* (Raise your hand, ask for clarification, etc.)

3. *"How do you feel when you want to know what to do, but there is too much talking to hear a certain voice?"* (Confused, lost, frustrated, alone, etc.)

4. *"What is a simple rule you can state about listening to directions?"* (When directions are being given, be quiet, still and listen.)

5. *" What signals could be used to show starting and stopping?"* (Tambourine, drum beat, bell.)

Directed Activity 2:

Direct another group of six to pantomime: *"Work in your own space to show how you are each a different zoo animal."* Personal space is enough area when one is in a stationary place to move the body without bothering another person.

Discussion (directed to players):

1. *"How did you feel having your own space in which to work?"*

2. *"What would happen if your neighbor got into your space?"*

3. *"Why is it important to respect a person's personal space?"*

4. *"How do you show that you care about a friend doing a job well?"* (By respecting the space in which one works.)

5. *"What rule can you state about personal space?"* (Your personal space is the area in which you have freedom to move without bothering another person.)

Directed Activity 3:

Direct another group of six to pantomime: *"You may choose to be an elf, a big tree, the sun, rain, a rainbow or a flower; each has a special thing to do."* Allow for improvisations.

Discussion (directed to players):

1. *"Remember your actions and feelings as we talk about what happened."* Discuss what happened sequentially; then have all of the children reflect their thoughts.

2. *"What rule can you state about sharing in Discussion Time?"* (When it is time for Discussion, remembering your own feelings and thoughts is important.)

3. *"What part of the elf story did you like most?"*

4. *"How could more characters have been added to make the story different?"*

5. *"What would you have changed to have a different ending?"*

6. *"What rule can you state about participating and sharing?"* (Play-acting, listening and sharing helps everyone to feel a part of the group, both players and audience. In creative drama, activities may be played or acted in many ways.)

Directed Activity 4:

Direct another group of six to pantomime horses in a parade, listening for the signal "freeze" to stop in place.

Discussion:

1. *"What happens when you hear 'freeze'?"*

2. *"What can you do to help someone follow the rules?"* (Provide reminder, encouragement, be a good example, etc.)

3. *"How does it help the group when everyone follows directions?"* (We can go onto next activity, all can hear, etc.)

4. *"What rule can you state about helping each other?"* (Encourage all in your group to do their best!)

5. *"If a person keeps moving even after hearing the signal, what happens?"*

6. *"How do you feel when someone interferes with what your are trying to do?"*

7. *"What rule can you state about consequences of not following directions?"* (When a person chooses to disobey a rule, that person chooses removal from the group.)

Summary:

Help the children learn that:

1. Participating through playing skills and audience skills creates group cooperation and a sense of belonging.

2. Listening to and following directions is necessary to do a job well, to feel good about one's self, and to have group cooperation.

3. Respect of personal space shows understanding of an individual's rights.

4. Being aware of and recalling one's own personal interpretations can produce idea-generation.

5. Mutual support to each group member strengthens the well-being of the whole class.

6. Lack of cooperation is a choice that results in a person's removal from the group.

Beginning Lesson 1.2

Be an Animal

Grades: K-8

Focus:

Imitative and interpretative movements and sounds, feelings, cause-effect

Introduction:

We can use our imagination to help us expand our knowledge about the world. In creative drama imagination is used in pretending to be animate objects, either animals or plants. The process of helping children to learn the difference between "animate" and "inanimate" categories is begun by pretending to be animals. Imagining what one would feel like and experience as an animal heightens sensitivity about animal life, habitats, conservation and care.

Preparation: Trotting Ponies

Warm-up. Going clockwise in a circle say, *"We shall walk on the count of one, two, three; then trot like ponies on four, five, six."* Repeat several times.

Cool-down. End with walking, then signal to move in slow motion, and get in a seated position.

Directed Activity:

Standing in a circle, introduce and model this idea: *"An animal can really be fun. Our imagination can help us be very little or extremely big. I will be an elephant.... My arm is my trunk.... I am large and my big legs and feet take much effort to move.... What things can an elephant do?"* (Children respond and join in the pretending, e.g., making sounds, drinking water, picking up peanuts, standing on a stool, walking in a circus ring.)

Direct children to become animals. *"Stay in your space and make sounds and movements to show your animals."* The facilitator leads in guessing what animals are represented.

Discussion:

The facilitator needs to model self-evaluating statements as, *"When I was an elephant, I really liked it!... I did not have to rush.... I could eat peanuts.... How do you think an elephant might feel?"* Children respond. They describe being specific animals that they portrayed. Questions may be:

1. *"Were you friendly, or unfriendly?"*
2. *"How would you want an owner to treat you?"*
3. *"Where would you live? In what other places could you live?"*
4. *"What was your family like?"*

Beginning Lesson 1.3

Be an Inanimate Object

Grades: K-8

Focus:

Imitative and interpretative movements and sounds, action-reaction

Introduction:

Our observational skills are increased as we imagine and "play out" what it is like being an inanimate object. Understanding for cause-effect relationships may be sharpened when we are involved in a specific process as an inanimate object.

Preparation: Ice-Skating

Warm-up. "We are on the ice and we are very good at skating.... We shall all go in a circle gliding along.... You may make spins or jumps, but mainly glide along, always keeping distance from each other."

Cool-down. "Now, we shall stop our skating and begin resting ourselves as we move in slow motion... coming to a halt, and being seated."

Directed Activity:

Standing in a circle, introduce and model this idea using movement and sounds: *"Being something that is not living, like a lamp, is fun.... I will be a lamp.... The switch must be on before I can give light.... I might make a room look pretty if I am a special lamp that is decorative... or I might be most useful if I am a lamp in a workshop.... Someone has just turned on the switch.... Electricity is going through my cord (arm), and now to the bulb (head).... If I could make a sound, it might be what?"* (Get sounds from class.)

Direct the children to become inanimate objects. *"Stay in your space and use your body and sounds to portray objects. These may be pencil sharpeners, boxes, desks, curtains, scissors, and crayons."* Encourage all kinds of motion extending from the three basic movements: twisting, bending and stretching.

Discussion:

Discuss body movements and sounds. The facilitator needs to model self-evaluative statements: *"When I was a lamp I liked giving out light.... It was nice to rest when the switch was off.... How could I have felt if I had been moved...?"* Children respond. Then they describe their own experiences.

Helping questions may be:

1. *"What did you like about being the object you chose?"*
2. *"How did you feel?"*
3. *"What did someone else do that was interesting?"*

Chapter II
Playing Skills

Sad, Mad, Glad, Bad, Lesson 2.3

Concentration: I Know What You Said

Grades: K-8

Focus:

Attending, recall, sharing

Introduction:

Concentration is the focus of the physical, mental and emotional processes in the presented activity. While focus is narrowed to a specific idea, the process also releases the body from physical stress so that mental and emotional openness happens.

Preparation: Swinging

Warm-up. *"Stretch by reaching up high, now drop arms, down to the ground as your legs bend; then push your body up with your legs and swing your arms in an upward direction; repeat and think how this is similar to being a swing. Add the sounds of the wind."*

Cool-down. *"Now quietly sit while listening to a secret the wind is telling you."*

Directed Activity:

In groups of six, children sit in circles on the floor and play the following game. Children are directed to sit quietly when another is talking and show that they are attending by using these behaviors:

Giving direct eye contact
Sitting still
Nodding head to show listening
Leaning forward to speaker
Thinking about what the speaker is saying

A child begins by stating one's own name and something fun that was done last week-end. The next child states one's own name and something fun done last week-end; then repeats the previous child's name and experience. The chain of information grows as each child repeats this process. When all have participated, each will be encouraged to repeat the complete chain of information. Each child is then given the opportunity to ask a question or make a comment directed to a particular student.

Discussion:

1. *"How does it feel for someone to listen to you?"*
2. *"Who did something that showed listening was happening? What was it?"*
3. *"How do you feel when you are called by your name?"*

Playing Skills 2.2

Sensory Awareness: Going to the Candy Store

Grades: K-8

Focus:

Seeing, hearing, feeling, tasting, thinking, perceiving

Introduction:

The five senses need to be identified and information from them collected in the memory of the student so that they can be used in creative drama. Sensory input is often the stimulation that evokes emotional responses and ideas. In creative drama activities, our five senses can help us learn more about our world.

Preparation: Music in My Ears

Warm-up. "Music, different tunes and rhythms give us patterns for moving.... Think of a fast song or music.... In a circle, let us show a fast movement to go with a fast tune... a slow movement for a slow tune."

Cool-down. "Now, change the music to slow, calm tunes.... Slow your movements... and now be still."

Directed Activity:

The class works individually in unison as the facilitator directs the activity. *"Pretend that you are going to a candy store. You shall choose a piece of your favorite candy.... As you walk in the door, what do you smell...? Cinnamon, chocolate, peppermint, licorice, coffee, strawberry.... What do you hear as you enter the candy store...? The cash register, conversation, cracking paper (candy-wrapper), container lids opening? See all the kinds of candy. What color and shape is the candy? In what type of container is the candy? Who is in the candy store? Choose the piece you want."*

Discussion:

1. *"How does it taste: sweet, sour, hot? Describe the flavor."*
2. *"How does it feel: hard, soft, crunchy, chewy?"*
3. *"What shape is it?"*
4. *"How else can you describe your piece of candy?"*
5. *"How do the people feel who work in the candy store?"*

Emotional Awareness: Sad, Mad, Glad, Bad

Grades: K-6

Focus:

Feelings, negative, positive influences

Introduction:

Emotional awareness is the basis for growing sensitivity to feelings within one's self and in others. Feelings are reflected in body movements, gestures, facial expression, verbalization and imitations. Rhythm, pitch and duration indicate the intensity of the emotions portrayed. Any one feeling can have a positive or negative aspect. All feelings are valid; responsibility for actions resulting from feelings must be assumed.

Preparation: Stormy Weather

Warm-up. *"Stand with your arms outstretched. With body movement and sound, make a form of a puffy cloud; now lightning... crashing thunder... now rain."*

Cool-down. *"Quietly, now, pretend that you are snow falling."*

Directed Activity:

Direct the class to work together, first showing these feelings by using body movements only, then showing feelings by using their voices also:

> sad (lonely, unhappy)
> mad (angry, upset)
> glad (joyful, happy)
> bad (guilty, afraid, scared)

Discussion:

1. *"What were the different ways our bodies appeared?"*

2. *"How did voice tones show feelings?"*

3. *"What 'pretend' feelings reminded you of a real situation you recall?"*

4. *"Which feelings are most pleasant?*

5. *"When can a bad or mad feeling be useful?"* (Helping one to become more determined to accomplish a goal; helping one to direct actions to improve a negative social situation, etc.)

6. *"What can happen when a person continues feeling negative emotions?"* (Emotions are contagious!)

7. *"What positive emotions are helpful at school?"* (determination, happiness, curiosity, etc.)

Movement: Moving In Our Own Space

Grades: K-8

Focus:

Body motion, pantomime

Introduction:

Movement is a basic building block of body expression and function. Children need physical movement to develop neurologically. Creative movement also facilitates language development. It is helpful to designate a child's space in which to work. Begin with small movements (e.g., hands making circles, head bobbing, feet tapping) then to larger movements within one's own working space. Distance in space, spatial relationships, levels of movements, pace and rhythm are all factors to be explored.

Preparation: Melting Ice Cream

Warm-up. "Standing, reach up high, then low. Now, pretend to be ice cream on a warm, windy day. Make a sound to show what is happening."

Cool-down. End with the signal to "freeze," then slowly lower the body to a seated position as a humming sound is made. When seated, sounds stop.

Directed Activity:

Emphasize everyone's need for personal body space in which to work while pantomiming these ideas. As a class, children are directed in these activities while standing:

> Twist to swing a baseball bat
> Turn head to look behind
> Stretch to reach a high shelf
> Reach a limb of a tree you are climbing
> Bend as a tree in the wind, a fishing line with a big fish on the hook

Discussion:

1. *"How does your body feel when it is twisting, stretching, reaching, bending?"*
2. *"Was anyone too close to you? Explain."*
3. *"Was anyone not close enough? Explain."*

Playing Skills 2.5

Imagination: Imagine That!

Grades: K-8

Focus:

Visual imagery, sensory recall, inventiveness

Introduction:

Imagination is the very essence of creative drama. The ability to "become" an inanimate object showing human characteristics gives enhanced perspectives. The ability to personify qualities, such as truth and freedom, allows children to better understand the concepts.

Preparation: Wings of Birds

Warm-up. "*Arms outstretched, now up, down, up, down; start moving around the circle like a bird flying high in the sky.... Think what kind of bird you are.*"

Cool-down. "*Now, become a swan on a calm river.... Float along with no sounds.... Now sit quietly.*"

Directed Activity:

Direct class to first use body movement and then put sounds to these:

A person in cave-dwelling days
An animal in the jungle
An inanimate object (e.g., rock, river, chair, spoon)

Discussion:

1. "*What was it like going to a different place?*"

2. "*What did you like doing the most?*"

3. "*Which was easiest for you to do? Hardest?*"

Playing Skills 2.6

Communication: Messages

Grades: K-8

Focus:

Body movement, gesture, tone and volume of voice

Introduction:

Communication is the process by which persons exchange information verbally and non-verbally. Voices can express many feelings: anger, I do not care, loneliness, love, hate and so forth.

Preparation: Twist and Bend

Warm-up. Lead with this rhyme as actions are added:
"Twist at the waist, to the left, to the right:
Bend to the toes, then stand upright."

Cool-down. *"Twist at the waist; turn around;*
Bend to your toes; then sit on the ground."

Directed Activity 1:

Children work in pairs to show different ways of communicating verbally or with sounds using these ideas:

> *"Come over here by me."*
> *"I will tell you a secret."*
> *"I like that."*

Discussion:

1. *"How did you feel when harsh tones were used? How did you feel when kind tones were used?"*

2. *"Which way of speaking did you like the most?"*

Directed Activity 2:

Using the same ideas, children pantomime messages. Explain that pantomime is communicating with the body only, no sounds or words are used.

Discussion:

1. *"Which form of communication is easiest to use? Which form is most difficult to use?"*

2. *"Which form of communication helped you feel special?"*

Playing Skills 2.7

Cooperation: Machine Magic

Grades: K-8

Focus:

Working together, dialogue, physical movement, idea-generation

Introduction:

Cooperation is the process of working together to help, enhance and encourage. Cooperation involves communication and willingness to understand people's needs.

Preparation: Flowers Opening

Warm-up. *"With our arms close to our bodies, kneeling down on the floor in a small ball, let us begin slowly growing like flowers.... Heads slowly up.... Arms as leaves.... Now we are fully grown and the wind is blowing.... Sway in the breeze."*

Cool-down. *"Now it is calm again.... Slowly calm your body movements as evening comes across the sky."*

Directed Activity:

In groups of five, children form a working machine. One part activates the next part, until the whole machine is doing its job. The machine parts must touch at least one other part, and all must make sounds and motions.

Discussion:

1. *"How did your group members work together?"*
2. *"Why is it important for each person to be responsible?"*
3. *"How does cooperation make a classroom run more smoothly?"*
4. *"Who needs to cooperate?"*
5. *"Who decides if you shall cooperate?"*

Chapter III
Playmaking Skills

Giants and Little Creatures, Lesson 3.4

Characterization: Hibernating Bears and Exuberant Clowns

Grades: K-8

Focus:

Physical mannerisms, movements, sounds, characterizations, voice

Introduction:

In characterization, the child builds an internal response to reflect particular qualities of the imagined person or thing. Pantomiming is a good beginning for building the emotions and actions of a character. Pantomiming frees children to release themselves into the "beings" that are created, whether animals, fantasy characters, humans or objects. The child's perspective can be seen through interpretative movement and characterization.

Preparation: Loose Arm Machine

Warm-up. *"Bend at the waist; let your arms drop gently, keep your feet still and twist from your waist while in a bending position. Add a b-z-z-z-z-z or other sound to add machine-like effect."*

Cool-down. *"Now, become a silent machine that folds up into a little ball on the floor... and now sit in a regular position."*

Directed Activity:

Children work in groups of six to experience being "big," using only movement and no sound; then "tiny." The facilitator comments about different representations and that variety is desired. Then the children pantomime a young colt in a field... a bear waking from hibernation... an exuberant clown.

Divide the class into four groups. Each member assumes a role in one of the situations listed below. Characterization is shown through the use of voice, body movement, facial expression and gestures. Each group presents its improvisation, while others act as the audience.

Situation 1 - farmer, plow, horse, gate, stone, snake
Situation 2 - baby, play-pen, doll, mother, father, sister
Situation 3 - teacher, student, new child, nurse, parent, neighbor
Situation 4 - elephant, clown, lion-tamer, lion, acrobat, trapeze artist

Discussion:

1. *"What did (child's name) do to show a character? How did words help?"*
2. *"What movements helped you know more about (child's name)?"*
3. *"How did (child's name) facial expressions show feelings?"*
4. *"What large body movements showed the character's intention? Small body movements?"*
5. *"How did (child's name) tone of voice express feelings?"*

Dialogue:
Happy Times, Happy Talk

Grades: K-8

Focus:

Words, tone of voice, conversation

Introduction:

Dialogue helps the characters and plot of a play to develop. It is the words said by the characters that help tell the story; and it reflects personal qualities of the characters.

Preparation: Mouse and Dinosaur

Warm-up. "Stand; with your body in motion, be a little mouse, add sounds; relax. Now with your body, be a gigantic dinosaur, add sounds."

Cool-down. "Back to being little, think of a tiny ladybug, and quietly sit down beside it."

Directed Activity:

Children work in groups of six. The facilitator directs them to begin a conversation based on an idea of animals and their "happy times." Each child becomes an animal and talks to the animal friends in the group. Children learn more about significant characterization through dialogue when they put movement and words together. They may wish to add sound effects for effectiveness. As children become more confident, other types of dialogue can be improvised in the following examples:

A bumblebee and a flower
A chair and a table
A worm and a rock
A cashier and a cash register
A lost child and a grocery clerk

Discussion:

1. *"Which example did you have the most fun doing?"*
2. *"Could some of the characters have had unhappy words?"*
3. *"How did you know someone was excited? Upset?"*
4. *"How does talking together help problems get solved?"*

Playmaking Skills 3.3
Plot: Sunken Treasure

Grades: 2-8

Focus: Plot, beginning, middle, ending, conflict, resolution

Introduction:

Plot is the series of related incidents in which characters act and react revealing a conflict and resolution in a logical sequence.

Preparation: Butterfly Catching

Warm-up. *"We are outside on a beautiful spring day.... Butterflies are everywhere.... We have nets on long poles.... We gently catch one to look at its beauty.... Think what it looks like."*

Cool-down. *"You are still looking at your butterfly.... Now you are letting it fly away as you gently release it from the net... up it goes; and now sit quietly."*

Directed Activity:

Groups of six improvise actions about a ship's crew, a sunken treasure and a shark. They use motions, sounds and words to develop a story which they present to other groups who act as the audience. After three minutes of planning time in which children decide their own parts, they are called into the larger group. The facilitator states that each story will probably be different and that the variety is desirable.... Everyone has good ideas.

Discussion:

After each group's story the facilitator asks:

1. *"What was the beginning of the story, the middle, the end?"*

2. *"How could something have happened differently?"*

3. *"What was the importance of the characters?"* (Characters help develop the conflict which is the core of the plot.)

4. *"How were the different incidents related?"*

5. *"How did sounds give information about the setting?"*

Theme or Idea: Giants and Little Creatures

Grades: 1-8

Focus:

Main idea, fact/non-fact

Introduction:

The theme is the main idea of the play. It forms as characters develop and interact in the plot.

Preparation: Stretch to Toes

Warm-up. *"Stretch your right arm and hand down to your left foot, then do the same with your opposite arm and foot; add machine sounds as you rotate sides."*

Cool-down. End with the signal to "freeze," then slowly drop the body to a seated position as a humming sound is made. When seated, sounds stop.

Directed Activity:

Lead children to imagine being a tree... an elf... ...a giant... and then a scared mouse. Children work in groups of six to improvise a story about an elf, giant, mouse and tree. A character or object can be made by several working together cooperatively. Allow three minutes, then all return to the large group for each improvisation to be presented. After each group, the facilitator leads the discussion.

Discussion:

1. *"What was the main idea of that group's story?"*
2. *"How did the characters help you know the idea?"*
3. *"How could the idea be presented differently?"*
4. *"What could have been fact?"*

Chapter IV
Belonging

Family Celebration, Lesson 4.3

Belonging 4.1

Friendship Squeeze

Grades: K-4

Focus:

Friendship, sensitivity to others, enthusiastic response, responsibility

Introduction:

A time to focus on an activity in which participants show caring and affectionate feelings enhances the sense of affiliation among group members.

Preparation: Swinging

Warm-up. *"Stretch by reaching up high, now drop arms, down to the ground as your legs bend; then push your body up with your legs and the momentum of swinging arms in an upward direction; repeat and think how this is similar to being a swing. Add the sounds of the wind."*

Cool-down. *"Now quietly sit while listening to a secret the wind is telling you."*

Directed Activity 1:

The children sit on the floor in a circle. Explain that everyone in this class is special and belongs; the circle is a "friendship circle" in which everyone plays an important role. Explain that the "friendship squeeze" will be passed around from one person to the next until it comes back to the originator. Ask the children what kind of a physical squeeze shows friendship i.e., firm, but gentle. Tell them to be silent and watch to see where the squeeze is, and applaud when the originator says, *"I got it!"*

Discussion:

1. *"What does a friendship circle mean to you?"*
2. *"Is there one person more important than another in the circle?"* (No.)
3. *"How would you feel if you were not included in the circle?"*

4. *"How did our body movements help us to feel like we belonged to the circle?"* (e.g., hand squeeze, eyes watching, bodies facing into circle.)

Directed Activity 2:

Ask a child to begin the squeeze, going counter-clockwise. This time think of a positive message to say aloud. (e.g., *"I am glad to be here"; "This is a super group"; "We are all important!"*)

Discussion:

1. *"How do our words help our actions in communicating?"*
2. *"How do you feel when someone shows enthusiasm?"*
3. *"How were messages alike? How were they different?"*
4. *"How did someone's message help you?"*
5. *"How does a friendship circle remind us of making others feel important?"*

Variations:

The children shut their eyes while sending around the squeeze silently.

Two children sit outside the circle while the squeeze is being passed; afterwards they tell their feelings about being outsiders.

Children divide into smaller groups to represent family roles; think of different messages the family members would send in a "caring squeeze."

Summary:

Help the children understand that:

1. All group members are equally important.
2. Persons feel a sense of belonging when they can participate in a group.
3. Body movements and voices help communicate sense of belonging.
4. Class members have the responsibility to be aware of each others' feelings.

Belonging 4.2

Smile Power Makes Others Flower

Grades: K-3

Focus:

Growth, cause-effect, environment, responsibility

Introduction:

Understanding that we have influence on and interdependence with others—both animals and plants—helps us see the importance of the behaviors we choose.

Preparation: Wings of Birds

Warm-up. *"Arms outstretched, now up, down, up, down; start moving around the circle like a bird flying high in the sky.... Think of what kind of bird you are."*

Cool-down. *"Now, become a swan on a calm river.... Float along with no sounds.... Now sit quietly."*

Directed Activity:

The children sit on the floor in a circle. Tell them that the "sun" is a designated student who will give "smile power," which will help them grow as plants of their own choice. Direct the "sun" to touch a child on the head to indicate direct sun rays to that child. The "seed" responds according to the amount of "smile power" given. A plant may grow profusely, or slowly. If the sun frowns, skies are cloudy and growth is slowed. All of the children have an opportunity to respond.

Discussion:

1. *"What kind of plant were you?"*
2. *"How did your size compare to others?*
3. *"How did you feel at different times?"*
4. *"What kinds of things could happen to you?"*
5. *"As a plant, what did you do that made you feel good?"*
6. *"What did others do that made you feel that you belonged?"*

7. *"In real life, how can we be helpful to plants?"*

8. *"How are plants and human beings alike in what they need?"*

9. *"Which plants were fast-growing; small, large; flowers, trees, and vegetables?"*

Variations:

The sun may give growing power by giving compliments.

Various weather conditions can be in a plot about plant growth.

Effect of population, industry, misuse of environment can add to this activity.

Summary:

Help the children understand that:

1. Plant life must have proper care to be healthy.

2. People and plants represent interdependency.

3. People and plants need nurturing.

4. Thoughtful acts produce growth; thoughtless behavior may lead to harmful effects.

Belonging 4.3
Family Celebration

Grades: 4-8

Focus:

Family roles, celebrations, cooperation, planning

Introduction:

Families are the support structure which provide nurturing and guidance to the young of the species. The family systems are the foundation of a society. If a society is to thrive and continue, families must be protected and strengthened.

Preparation: Magic Family Auto

Warm-up. "Stand; get inside a magic automobile that is very tiny.... Now, as you think of special family members you want with you, you and the car get bigger and bigger."

Cool-down. "Now, you magically arrive at your favorite place; you and your family are quietly waiting for a surprise as you sit down."

Directed Activity:

Divide the class into three groups. "*Your group shall pretend to be a family in another country. It is a family with very strong ties, and the members living in your house include parents, grandparents, sisters, brothers, aunts, uncles and cousins.*" Direct groups to have a family meeting to discuss plans for an upcoming celebration, special event or holiday which will be enacted for other groups. Allow three minutes for planning. Then each group presents to others who serve as the audience. These ideas should be addressed:

What will the special event be? (e.g., birth of new baby, victory over another tribe, New Year, coming of spring.)

How will you, as a family, celebrate it? (e.g., customs, foods, decorations, music dance, costumes, religious activities.)

Who will explain the importance of the event to children?

What is to be done in making preparations for the event?

Who will do each job?

How many roles do you have in your "family"? (e.g., A boy is son to a father, brother to sibling, etc.)

Discussion:

1. *"What was your job and how did you feel about it?"*
2. *"How were different ages represented? What were the different responsibilities relating to age?"*
3. *"How did it feel to be in your family? Why?"*
4. *"What would happen if someone did not do one's job in a specific role?"*
5. *"What have you learned in this experience that is helpful to you in understanding the importance of families?"*

Variations:

Children from different cultures share their traditions. Groups develop plots for story endings which are supplied by the facilitator.

Summary:

Help the children understand that:

1. People who help each other feel a sense of belonging.
2. Families, groups, and societies pass traditions from one generation to another.
3. In a specific family there are many roles; one person plays several roles.
4. When a job is not done by a specific member, it is shifted to another person who does the job, or it is neglected.

Belonging 4.4

Favorite Childhood Experience

Grades: K-8

Focus:

Recall of sensory and emotional experience, concentration, stress reduction, pantomime

Introduction:

Recall of special memories is one way to foster a relaxed mental state and to allow for the development of new insights. The sharing of favorite experiences helps to build positive climate within a classroom or group.

Preparation: Movement and Voice

Warm-up. *"Stand; with your body in motion, show the feeling of being afraid; now, be brave. Relax. Think how sounds can add to show those feelings. Let us add sounds to body movements and show the feelings of surprise; now, disappointment."*

Cool-down. *"Now, remember a quiet happy time, and sit down calmly."*

Directed Activity 1:

Ask the children to recall a favorite experience from earlier years by quietly sitting with their eyes closed as these suggestions are made to stimulate memory:

A special family event
A favorite person
A happy time
A special holiday

Allow thirty seconds between each suggestion for reflective memory.

Directed Activity 2:

For K-3, each child has a turn to pantomime one's own special memory for the class. For 3-8, divide the class into groups of six; each child has a turn to pantomime one's own special memory within the small group while group members guess what is represented. After three minutes, the groups sit down and talk among their members about their special memories. Direct the class to come together to share the feeling words.

Discussion:

1. *"What kinds of memories are similar?"*
2. *"How are special memories important?"*
3. *"When are some difficult times that good memories can be helpful?"*
4. *"How do good memories help build positive thoughts?"*

Variations:

A favorite story can be recalled.
Favorite characters in history can be recalled.
An adventurous experience can be recalled.

Summary:

Help the children understand that:

1. Good memories help build a positive sense of belonging and self-esteem.
2. The power to retrieve a good memory helps a person feel self-control, and reduces stress build-up.
3. Good memories can be recalled to replace a negative memory.

Belonging 4.5

Frontier Spirit

Grades: K-8

Focus:

Interdependence, families, life skills, personal qualities, cooperation

Introduction:

When we can identify with others in a sense of commonalty, we feel a connectedness. Linking up with historical figures and times helps children to better understand the relationships of past and present. By imagining what future roles they may have, they gain an understanding of their part in creating rootedness for others.

Preparation: Time Machine

Warm-up. *"Stand; get inside the time machine.... You have to fill it up completely by expanding yourself as much as you can."*

Cool-down. *"Now, decrease in size and become microscopic as you sit on the floor."*

Directed Activity:

Discuss the concept of "frontier," a place not well-known or explored. *"Long ago frontiers were just beyond a cave, or the other side of an ocean. We will become adventurers in the past. As we step into our time machine, we are able to go back to days of the early settlers."*

Depending on age of children and subject content that is being studied, a particular historical setting can be designated. Divide the children into groups of six, each group being assigned specific tasks to incorporate in their improvisation from this list:

> Gather food; build a fire
> Hunt wild game; make tools and weapons
> Build homes; plant crops
> Care for family members; teach children
> Communicate with neighbors; with distant friends
> Drive a wagon; trade for supplies
> Share family traditions; share village celebration

Allow three minutes for group work. Half of the groups present their ideas while the others serve as the audience; then reverse. Direct the class in improvising "A Day on the Frontier" using parts of each group's presentation. Serve as narrator while groups listen to cues for action. When a group is not providing the main action, it may help with sound effects.

Discussion:

1. *"How did it feel to live long ago?"*
2. *"How are we like those pioneers? How are we different?"*
3. *"How was cooperation shown in the family? How was cooperation shown in the village?"*
4. *"What hardships made life difficult then? How did pioneers deal with these hardships?"*
5. *"What do you do when you have a hardship or problem today?"*
6. *"How do those same qualities help us today?"*

Variations:

These ideas can also be used for improvisation:

A Day in My Teen Age Years
A Day in My Adult Life
A Day in My Life as a Grandparent
A Day in the Future Environment in 2050

Summary:

Help the children understand that:

1. People live interdependently with others and in the environment.
2. When people help each other, they feel a sense of belonging.
3. Families transmit their behaviors and values through ways they live.
4. The frontier spirit embraces qualities of mental, emotional and physical strengths.

Good Feelings Museum

Grades: K-8

Focus:

Body language, feelings, cooperation

Introduction:

We like to feel good when we are in work or leisure settings. Focusing on positive emotions during a group task helps in building a healthy climate for caring and cooperation.

Preparation: High, Low

Warm-up. This may be put to a rhythm or tune and repeated. Use motions. *"Reach up high, then down low, Clap your hands and around you go!"*

Cool-down. Repeat the rhyme ending with "down you go!" indicating to sit quietly.

Directed Activity:

Discuss what kinds of things can be seen in a museum (e.g., paintings, sculptures, dioramas, old books.) Lead the class in thinking about going into a "Good Feelings Museum" where sculptures represent many positive feelings. Divide the children into groups of six. All groups have one minute to form a group sculpture representing the feeling "happy." Each member must link to another person. Allow groups to observe the others; discuss similarities, differences. Then the groups choose words to represent sculpture.

> excited
> proud
> eager
> self-confident
> loved
> determined
> courageous
> courteous
> safe

Discussion:

1. *"How did your group work together?"*
2. *"How were different body levels used?"*
3. *"What did you like in other groups?"*
4. *"How do these ideas help us know more about feelings?"*

Variation:

Sculptures can represent a variety of concepts as inventions, space exploration, animal families, music, etc. Sculptures may "come to life" with movement and sound. The facilitator may begin dialogue with the "sculpture" leading in spontaneous comments from group members. Each sculpture group may form a story to act or write.

Summary:

Help the children understand that:

1. Cooperation creates a sense of belonging.
2. Positive feelings include many kinds of responses.

Belonging 4.7

Director and Cast

Grades: 3-8

Focus:

Compliments, participation, responsibility, leadership, cooperation, applause

Introduction:

Being a part of a selected group which performs a special task which is recognized by others helps us to feel a sense of belonging and success. Additional positive reinforcement occurs when appreciation is demonstrated.

Preparation: Sounds All Around

Warm-up. "Stand very still. Listen to the sounds all around. Pick out one to pantomime." (Example: car outside—student pretends to be driving; pencil sharpener—student pretends to be using sharpener.) *"Each person, stay in your place and show what you hear, then add sounds."*

Cool-down. "Now, pretend all sounds stop, and as you sit, think of silence."

Directed Activity:

Children sit on the floor in a circle. Tell them to pass around an object. At the sound of a specific signal from the facilitator (tambourine, drum-beat, etc.), the object is held. The one who has the object goes to the middle of the circle and becomes the "director" for five others who are picked by the facilitator to work as the "cast." They improvise an idea that is chosen by the "director." (The list can be on the board, on cards, or verbally presented. For younger children, more direction is given by the facilitator than by the child "director.") The director's job is to encourage everyone to participate and cooperate, and to compliment their actions, words, characterization and so forth. The director may give suggestions to the "cast" as they improvise one of these ideas:

An old man and grandchild going fishing
And elephant in an ant bed
A three-story house in a tornado
A family of butterflies about to migrate
A foreign student new to a community

Creative Drama

When the improvisation is concluded, the "director" compliments each player and the circle members applaud. The circle game resumes; a new "director" and "cast" continues the procedure. All children should have a chance to be in the circle before anyone has a second turn.

Discussion:

1. "How did you feel being in the circle? Being director?"
2. "What parts were fun to watch? To do?"
3. "How does giving and receiving compliments help a person to feel that one belongs?"
4. "What could happen to cause a cast not to want to work together?"
5. "How are good leaders and followers alike?"
6. "How does applause show appreciation?"

Variation:

Groups demonstrate specific concepts being studied e.g., rotation, revolution; plant growth addition, subtraction. Improvisation can be done with no sounds.

Summary:

Help the children understand that:

1. All group members are equally important.
2. Persons feel they belong to a group when they can do something well, and when they are recognized for their efforts.
3. A good leader helps strengthen others through compliments and encouragement.
4 A good leader gives responsibility to others.

Belonging 4.8

When Things Change (Loss)

Grades: K-6

Focus:

Stages of the grief process: shock, denial; sadness, anger, guilt, acceptance

Introduction:

Any significant change that is experienced as a loss can diminish self-esteem and sense of belonging. A family move may produce loss of friends, insecurity at school and questions of abilities. The loss of a pet may cause acute pain and anger. The death of a friend or family member usually results in the full range of stages in the grief process, though the time for experiencing each stage varies with individuals. Expressing feelings of loss enables the griever to better understand the feelings. It allows those around to simplify the healing process if they understand the necessity for the grief stages. When a loss is felt, memory of past losses may come to the forefront; events that normally would not cause concern may become magnified. By helping children understand that many kinds of changes happen, they are more equipped to deal effectively. Much sensitivity on the facilitator's part is required for this activity.

Preparation: Push the Walls Away

Warm-up. *"Stand; take two deep breaths; now 'push' the walls away, relax; now 'push the ceiling up,' relax."* (Repeat once using sounds to show exertion.)

Cool-down. *"Your arms need to rest; let them quietly pull your body weight down to a sitting position."*

Directed Activity 1:

Tell the class that this activity is to help them to understand about sadness and serious feelings. Divide the class into four groups to improvise situations showing feelings of loss. Allow three minutes. Each group presents its situation as others serve as the audience. These ideas may be improvised:

A mother tells her son his dog got run over.
A neighbor is a best friend; her family is moving.

A boy is told he must move into another class.
A favorite teacher is ill and will not be coming back to school this year.
A child has a disease and cannot play outside

Discussion:

1. *"How did the group show sad or upset feelings?"*
2. *"What did you feel as you were in your group's presentation? As an audience member?"*
3. *"What could help you feel better if you were really having upset feelings?"*
4. *"What could you do to help a friend if your friend was really having those feelings?"* (Young children often say they would give a friend their toys, candy, etc. It is important to help them understand that being a friend means letting the hurting person talk and that being a good listener is important; that encouraging the hurting person to talk to a caring adult can be helpful.)

Reinforce that feelings are real, and that it is all right to have bad feelings. It is important to know how to change actions to change feelings. This does not mean that crying or fear should be suppressed. It is a focus to provide positive closure for this activity.

Directed Activity 2:

Direct the children to use expressive voices as they make these statements.

"To change my feelings, I will change my action."

"To be happy, I will act happy.... The feeling will follow."

"To be cooperative, I will act cooperative.... The feeling will follow."

"To be enthusiastic, I will act enthusiastic."

Discussion:

"How does a decision to make changes in bad feelings help a person?"

Variations:

The same activity is done with a more limited focus as in these situations:

A child is dreading a hospital stay.

A class is preparing for the return of a member after that person has suffered the personal loss. (e.g., death of family member, house that has burned, etc.)

Summary:

Help the children understand that:

1. All kinds of negative feelings may be experienced when a change or loss happens.
2. It is all right to have bad feelings; it is not all right to continue to keep them.
3. It is important to know ways to change bad feelings (e.g., express feelings by crying, talking, holding something soft, working with clay or crayons.)
4. Feelings of loss must be dealt with in order to begin the healing process.

Chapter V
Power

Tree-Top Land, Lesson 5.8

Power 5.1

Body Communication

Grades: K-8

Focus:

Communication, emotions, body movements, facial expressions.

Introduction:

Body language is a more powerful communicator than the content of the message. It is said that the content of the message accounts for less than 35% of the message received.

Preparation: Hopping

Warm-up. "Stand, get ready to hop around the circle. Think of all kinds of things that hop, and as we begin, pretend to be one of those things."

Cool-down. End with the signal to "freeze," then in slow motion, "float" down to a seated position.

Directed Activity 1:

The children sit on the floor in a circle. Direct the children to think of ways that hands can communicate to show comfort, signals, giving, saying "hi" and "help." *"We will take turns going around the circle. Communicate a certain emotion or message to the neighbor on your right. Then your neighbor will guess what feeling or message you are showing or giving. Remember, use your hands only!"* Continue around the circle until all have had a turn.

Discussion:

"How do motions talk and give measages?"
"How can hand signals be misinterpreted?"

Directed Activity 2:

Direct the children to think how their eyes can show shock, surprise, sadness, happiness, disinterest, anger and fear. In a circle, direct the students to communicate to the person on their right a specific feeling using their eyes only. The neighbor then guesses what the feeling is. Continue around the circle until all have a turn.

Discussion:

1. *"How are eyes important in letting us know how a person feels?"*

2. *"What eye expressions did you like most?"*

Directed Activity 3:

Direct the children to think how the whole body communicates silently with posture, facial expression and movement. One-third of the class stands; the others serve as the audience. Direct the children who are standing to show how they would feel in these situations:

Your report card has much higher grades than you thought it would have.

Your mother has just told you that you are going to take a special vacation.

You have just heard there will be no school on Monday.

Discussion:

"How do the bodies look when happy feelings are shown; when surprised feelings are shown?"

Directed Activity 4:

Direct another third of the class to show with body communication how they would feel in these situations:

Little brother has just torn up your homework paper.

Your neighbor borrows pencils without asking you.

Someone accuses you of doing something you did not do.

Think of a time when you were very angry and let your body show it.

Discussion:

"How do the people's bodies look when upset feelings are shown; when angry feelings are shown?"

Directed Activity 5:

Direct the last third of the class to show with body communication how they would feel in these situations:

Your pet has been hurt.

Your best friend has moved away.

You have hurt yourself and you will not be able to play in your soccer game.

Discussion:

1. *"How do people's bodies look when sadness or disappointment is shown?"*
2. *"What are some other feelings the human body can show?"* (e.g., Tired, sick, afraid, lonely, proud. satisfied.)

Summary:

Help the children understand that:

1. Body position and movement can send messages.
2. Facial expressions and eyes can show emotions.

Power 5.2

Hot Air Balloon

Grades: K-8

Focus:

Imagination, sensory and emotional awareness, transportation

Introduction:

When we see the "whole picture," we can better understand interdependency. Awareness of the world around us, the people and processes can sharpen our vision in solving problems.

Preparation: Humming Twist

Warm-up. "Standing, twist slowly from your waist up; keep moving your shoulders, head, and eyes as far as you can go. Now, to the opposite side. Repeat three times. Make humming sounds going from side to side."

Cool-down. End with the signal to "freeze," then slowly drop your body to a seated position as a humming sound is made. When seated, sounds stop.

Directed Activity:

The children stand in a circle. Direct them to take on the role of voyagers in the balloon. *"We are preparing to take an imaginary journey in a hot air balloon. We shall blow the balloon up as we make a large circle; let us get tight together and, as you hear 'more helium,' move slowly outward to show that the balloon is getting bigger and rising. Listen for 'stop.' As you hear 'release,' the helium is going out of a small opening in the top of the balloon and as it gets smaller, we make the circle smaller. The balloon lowers when the helium is released."* Practice getting the circle bigger, then smaller; going up, then down.

The facilitator narrates the questions: *"We are floating above houses.... What do they look like? Now we are going over a highway and there is much traffic.... What is it like?"* Continue with several other suggestions of the country side, bodies of water, different elevations. *"What kinds of animals are there?"* Accept all answers. Bring the journey to an end by releasing the helium, lowering slowly to a safe spot. A vehicle and driver have followed along to pick up the children and the balloon to return to their starting point.

Discussion:

1. *"What were your feelings as we began going up?"*
2. *"How was being up high different from being on the ground?"*
3. *"How does traveling help us learn more?"*
4. *"How does 'getting a bigger picture' help us understand more?"*
5. *"How does the area look different compared to fifty years ago?"*
6. *"How does balloon travel compare to other forms of transportation?"*
7. *"In what ways do you feel powerful when you use transportation?"*

Variations:

Take a mental journey in a balloon for relaxation.

Take a journey in a balloon to do cartography or map-making.

Summary:

Help the children understand that:

1. There are many factors that influence quality of life.
2. Man and environment affect each other.
3. Transportation gives a sense of power when a person can go from one place to another.

Power 5.3

I Am A Terrific Person

Grades: K-8

Focus:

Self-confidence, positive self-talk, gestures

Introduction:

The importance of knowing one's competence, positive qualities and ability to solve problems gives a person a feeling of power. When we consciously build an understanding of our strengths and know how to increase them in appropriate ways, we develop personal confidence.

Preparation: Mouse and Dinosaur

Warm-up. "*Stand; with your body in motion, be a little mouse, add sounds; relax. Now with your body, be a gigantic dinosaur, add sounds.*"

Cool-down. "*Back to being little, think of a tiny ladybug, and quietly sit down beside it.*"

Directed Activity 1:

"*Today we will demonstrate ways to be friendly and kind with words and body movements.*" Direct half of the class to demonstrate for the other half who serves as audience; then reverse. Lead the children by modeling friendly actions and words. Examples are listed:

> Greeting a friend
> Complimenting someone
> Offering to help carry things
> Including friends in play
> Meeting a new neighbor
> Giving a hug

Discussion:

1. "*What showed caring? Helpfulness?*"

2. "*How did different persons show friendliness?*"

3. "*How did tones of voice and words show that a person was feeling confident? Enthusiastic? Determined?*"

Directed Activity 2:

Direct the class to think about situations which happen that result in feelings of being unloveable and uncaring (e.g., someone laughs at you, takes your supplies, calls you "dumb", hits). *"When such things happen, it is important to remember good messages about yourself like, 'I am loveable and capable!' and to remember that 'I am doing well!' Even when you make mistakes, you need to say, 'Okay, I made a mistake, but I will keep on doing my best! I will do better the next time'."*

Direct the class to pantomime things they like to do (e.g., playing at the park, fishing, swimming). Then pretend that something happens to cause a problem. *"Show how your feelings are pulling you down.... Now, think of a good message to say to yourself.... Put gestures or actions with your message to show enthusiasm and determination."*

These are some suggestions:

"I am loveable and capable!" (pointing to self, smiling)

"I can do it!" (emphasizing words)

"I am a good friend." (patting neighbor's back, smiling)

"Being happy is a good habit." (pretending to do school work, then looking satisfied)

"To be happy, act happy!" (smiling, standing tall, waving to a friend)

Discussion:

1. *"How do you feel when you cannot do something well? Or, when you are laughed at?"*

2. *"Positive self-talk helps to change feelings. What are some good messages you can say often to yourself?"*

3. *"When are times you can help a friend to learn about the power of good self-talk?"*

Summary:

Help the children understand that:

1. Positive self-talk can help turn negative feelings into positive feelings.

2. A reservoir of positive messages is useful to have at all times to give a person a sense of power.

Power 5.4

Body and Voice Messages

Grades: K-8

Focus:

Communication, needs, assertiveness, self-confidence

Introduction:

Three ways to act, and speak when communicating with someone are in the manner of a shy, a bossy or an assertive person. We communicate these different ways through tone of voice, body position, eyes and facial expressions.

Preparation: Frowns and Clowns

Warm-up. "Our faces, bodies, and voices tell our feelings. First, let us look very sad... now, happy.... Silently be a clown with definite movements as we go around in a circle."

Cool-down. "Now, calmly be a clown in slow motion... and go back to your space very quietly."

Directed Activity:

The facilitator demonstrates the three communication models by saying to a student, *"Can you come to my house to visit?"* Each time, body and voice reflect different qualities:

Shy (looking down at the floor, hanging head, almost inaudible and barely using any verbal communication)

Bossy person (loud, grabbing at student, hands on hips)

Assertive person (looks other person in the eye, calls other person by name, friendly, thoughtful, enthusiastic)

Direct students to sit on the floor in a circle. Tell the students that each of them will have a turn being the "speaker" inviting the student on their right to join in playing a game using one of the three methods just shown. The person on the right, the "listener," will decide which method is used and check with the speaker to verify if the guesses were correct. Continue around the circle until each student has had a turn.

Discussion:

1. *"How did you feel when a person used the shy method of invitation?"*

2. *"How did you feel when the bossy method was used?"*

3. *"How did you feel when the direct or assertive method was used?"*

Summary:

Help the children understand that:

1. A person using the shy method of communication usually does not have one's needs met. That person does not feel satisfied. A person who receives the shy communication feels uncomfortable, maybe angry, and has little respect for the shy person.

2. The bossy person may get needs met for the moment, but the person acted upon feels uncomfortable and might reject the bossy person or retaliate.

3. Persons using the direct, assertive method feel a sense of self-direction; they are satisfied that they have stated their needs. The person acted upon is free to respond effectively to the other person in the way chosen. Neither feels less power because of the other person.

Creative Drama

Power 5.5

Word Messages

Grades: K-8

Focus:

Assertiveness, needs, communication, self-confidence

Introduction:

People have the right to express themselves while respecting the rights of others; they have the right to ask for fair treatment and to defend themselves. In stating an "I message," the speaker uses this formula:

Example:

I + get angry + when you laugh at me + will you please stop.
   (what you   (what the   (what you need or
   are feeling)   problem is)   want to happen)

When we give an 'I message,' we feel that we can make good choices and decisions. If we can understand the process of the assertive method, then we can choose a very effective form of communication.

Preparation: Twist and Bend

Warm-up. Lead with this rhyme as actions are added:
*"Twist at the waist, to the left, to the right:
Bend to the toes, then stand upright."*

Cool-down. *"Twist at the waist; turn around;
Bend to your toes; then sit on the ground."*

Directed Activity 1:

The children work in two lines facing each other showing the differences between shy and bullying behaviors. Line A members tell Line B that they like strawberry ice cream using "shy" body movements and voices.

Discussion:

1. *"Line B, how do you feel about the way Line A communicated? Why?"*

2. *"Line A members, how did you feel giving that message in a shy way?"*

Directed Activity 2:

Have Line B give the same message to Line A in a "bullying" manner. Repeat the discussion questions. Lines reverse the "shy" and "bully" roles in these situations:

A person cuts in front of you in the cafeteria and you do not like it.

You want to ask your parent if a friend can come to play.

Discussion:

1. *"How do you feel when you use a shy or whimpering voice? When somebody else does?"*

2. *"Do you really want to help the person with the little voice?"*

3. *"Is that person going to get what is wanted?"*

4. *"What would be a better way for your body and voice to give a message?"* (Ask some questions about bullying behaviors.)

Directed Activity 3:

"When we talk about a problem, it is important to stand tall, speak up, look the person in the eye, and make our statement in a matter-of-fact voice. The best way to communicate when we need something is to use an 'I message.' Think of a message you would like to give to someone." (e.g., 'I want to see a movie,' 'do not lean against my desk.') *"Practice using the 'I message' with a partner."*

Discussion:

Help children understand that:

1. Shy persons do not get what they want, and usually do not feel good about themselves.

2. The person to whom the shy person talks is uncomfortable with the interaction.

3. Bullies may get their way, but the persons they deal with feel uncomfortable about the interactions.

4. The "I message" is a healthy, clear way to communicate.

5. Being assertive helps a person to see needs and make choices.

Power 5.6

Scary Dream

Grades: K-8

Focus:

Fear, fact versus non-fact, coping skills

Introduction:

Knowing how to manage feelings of fear helps us to feel a sense of power. Understanding and practicing fear-reduction techniques can help in building a repertoire of stress-reducing behaviors.

Preparation: Magic Family Auto

Warm-up. *"Stand; get inside a magic automobile that is very tiny... now, as you think of special family members that you want with you, you and the car get bigger and bigger."*

Cool-down. *"Now, you magically arrive at your favorite place; you and your family are quietly waiting for a surprise as you sit down."*

Directed Activity 1:

Discuss what comes to mind when thinking of a scary dream (e.g., big wind, monster, frightening sounds, shadows). Children work in groups of six to create a scary dream to present to other groups. (No killing or violence to others may be portrayed.) Remind them that movement and sounds represent actions and feelings and that people may work together to form one animal or object. Allow two minutes for group work.

Discussion:

"How did you feel when you were watching that dream?"
"How did you feel when you were taking part in your group's dream?"

Directed Activity 2:

Children work as a class to "get rid of" the bad dream. Standing collectively, the class group represents a bad dream; the students gather close together, taking up as little space as possible. The facilitator tells them that when a certain signal is given, they will spread out and then "freeze" when that word is said; at that time, the bad dream will no longer exist...it will be dispelled.

Discussion:

1. *"What are some other ways to get rid of a scary dream?"* (e.g., pretend to stomp it out; draw it; cut it into pieces; and throw it away.)

2. *"What can be done to keep from having a scary dream repeated?"* (Mentally replace it with a good dream before going to sleep.)

Summary:

Help the children understand that:

1. People do not have to be over-powered by bad dreams or fears.

2. People can take control of the dream and get rid of it.

3. Talking about a fear will tend to make it less frightening.

Power 5.7

Thirty-Second Vacation

Grades: 1-8

Focus:

Stress reduction, mental imagery, sensory awareness, pantomime

Introduction:

Mental imagery can be a powerful tool. Facilitators should be cautious to allow children to close eyes in a relaxed atmosphere with no hint that something is "wrong" if they cannot get a mental picture. Also, this type of activity should be for a few seconds, not a series of several minutes, especially when first done. A calm voice is important in beginning the activity, and in initiating comments after the imagery process.

Preparation: Swinging

Warm-up. *"Stretch by reaching up high, now drop arms, down to the ground as your legs bend; then push your body up with your legs and swing your arms in an upward direction; repeat and think how this is similar to being a swing. Add the sounds of the wind."*

Cool-down. *"Now quietly sit while listening to a secret the wind is telling you."*

Directed Activity:

Direct the class to "prepare for a mental journey," a thirty-second vacation, imagining where they would like to be. Tell them that when it is time for the vacation, they shall be quiet, still and close their eyes. When the "vacation" is ended, they will open their eyes and remain quiet to remember details. The facilitator's voice indicates when the journey begins and ends.

Children sit quietly and comfortably with their eyes closed. With a calm voice say, *"Think of a place you would really like to be.... See yourself there.... Think what you see.... What can you smell...? Hear...? Is there something to eat...? What colors and shapes are there...? What are you doing?"* Notice the children's responses; some will smile and move their bodies, while others may give no visible clues. After thirty seconds say, *"And now... come back to this place."*

Some children may have difficulty "seeing" anything the first few times. It is important that the facilitator assure the class that this is like any other skill; the more it is practiced, the sharper it becomes. Children often enjoy sharing about their vacations, but the teacher should not insist on sharing aloud.

These are some ways to hasten sharing:

Groups of four share with each other through pantomiming. Group members may ask others to help act certain parts.

Those who saw animals become those characters.
Those who were with family members show what happened.
Those who experienced food show what happened.
Those who were in a fantasy place, show what happened.

Discussion:

1. *"If you were able to see a picture, did it give you a good feeling?"*

2. *"Think of ways it can be fun to take a 'mental vacation'."*

3. *"A short 'vacation' gives you a break, a few moments to relax. When are some times this would help you relax?"* (before a test, during an assignment if tension is building, when fear is experienced, etc.)

4. *"Let us name the kinds of things to recall that help many people to relax."* (water, furry animals, green places, fire in a fireplace, being with family members or friends, etc.)

Variations:

Groups may portray a combination of "vacations," taking ideas for setting, action, and characters from different group members and synthesizing into a plot.

Mental imagery may be used to study a historical period in gathering sensory information.

Summary:

Help the children understand that:

1. Changing thought-patterns of stress or fear gives a person a sense of power.
2. Taking a mental journey can produce more ideas.
3. A person can learn some ways to control stress.
4. Taking a mental journey can replace sadness and discouragement.

Power 5.8

Tree-Top Land

Grades: K-6

Focus:

Mental imagery, sensory awareness, stress reduction, taking turns, safety rules

Introduction:

Simple physical activities can help us to feel in control and able to manage daily stress. When combined with pleasant sensory impressions and positive emotions, our sense of well-being is enhanced.

Preparation: Stretch to Toes

Warm-up. *"Stretch your right arm and hand down to your left foot, then do the same with opposite arm and foot; add machine sounds as you rotate sides."*

Cool-down. End with the signal to "freeze," then slowly drop your body to a seated position as a humming sound is made. When seated, sounds stop.

Directed Activity:

The children sit in a circle. *"Today we shall travel to tree-top land in a swing. Close your eyes and pretend you are swinging.... Look at all the things you see.... Now open your eyes and stand with a partner. One will push the other in an imaginary swing, and then you will change places. Let us remember about safety rules."*

Children work in pairs taking turns. Return to the circle and prepare to swing in their own special swings. While "swinging," suggest that they will swing up high, be safe, and get a view of tree tops. Ask these questions while swinging happens:

"How does the air feel or, smell?"
"What do you hear while swinging?"
"What does your swing look like?"
"Is it a long or short swing? How is it attached?"
"What kinds of feelings do you have while swinging?"

"Now have your swing be in a beautiful meadow where there are many plants and small animals.... What do you see?"
"How does it feel to be there?"
"What are you thinking about as you swing?"

Discussion:

1. *"Why do people swing?"*
2. *"What other things can you do while swinging?"*
3. *"How does swinging give you a sense of power?"*

Variations:

"Swing" over a negative social interaction like a fight on the playground to get the "whole picture" to understand what was happening.

For stress reduction without moving, help children use visualization by mentally "swinging."

Summary:

Help the children understand that:

1. Simple childhood activities provide sensory enjoyment and imagination when recalled.
2. Body movement, both real and imagined, can give a sense of relaxation and enjoyment.
3. Persons can learn ways to relax and to feel in control of their bodies.

Chapter VI

Uniqueness

Spotlight. Lesson 6.4

Uniqueness 6.1

My Special Place

Grades: K-8

Focus:

Imagination, stress reduction, sensory awareness

Introduction:

We need to experience relaxation techniques so that we can gain knowledge in how to use them when our bodies signal tiredness, fear or frustration.

Preparation: Ice-Skating

Warm-up. *"We are on the ice and we are very good at skating.... We shall all go in a circle gliding along.... You may make spins or jumps. but mainly glide along. always keeping distance from each other."*

Cool-down. *"Now. we will stop our skating and begin resting ourselves as we move in slow motion... coming to a halt. and being seated."*

Directed Activity 1:

Direct the children to sit in a circle and prepare to ride a magic carpet that will take them wherever they want to go. *"Take two deep breaths.... Close your eyes. and imagine that you are riding over clouds... over meadows... over tree-tops. Now. come back to this place landing gently... and you are here in the circle again. Open your eyes."*

Discussion:

"As you rode on the carpet. what was it like?" (Assure children that it is all right if imagery did not happen.)

Directed Activity 2:

"Take two deep breaths.... Now close your eyes. Let us pretend that just as the school day begins. the principal announces on the loud speaker that today there will be no school.... Very calmly, get on a magic carpet and go to a favorite spot anywhere you would like to be. Use your wonderful imagination to

see where you are.... Hear sounds... Smell odors.... Experience tastes.... Look to see what is around your special place." Allow about thirty seconds; then say, *"As you are still seeing your special place, think of two or three words that describe how you feel being there... and now, open your eyes."*

Discussion:

1. *"What special feelings did you have?"*

2. *"What did you hear? Smell? Taste?"*

3. *"What was your special place like?"*

4. *"How can you use body movements and sounds to show what your special place was like?"*

Directed Activity 3:

Direct the children to show in their own space what their special place is like using body movements and sounds. Encourage them to characterize. Circulate to guide the ones who are having difficulty.

Discussion:

1. *"How can remembering your special place be helpful?"* (e.g., when there is worry, fear, frustration, tiredness.)

2. *"How does your wonderful imagination help you?"* (e.g., takes you places you have never been, can take you back or forward in time, etc.)

Summary:

Help the children understand that:

1. Imagination is a useful tool to help overcome difficulties.

2. When the body signals tiredness, fear or frustration, mental imagery can alleviate the feeling.

3. Relaxation techniques are effectively used throughout working periods to enhance personal comfort and increase intellectual learning.

4. Persons feel special when they can create an imaginary event or place.

Uniqueness 6.2

If Pictures Could Talk

Grades: K-8

Focus:

Concentration, sensory awareness, imagination, interdependency

Introduction:

Imagination can transport us to small places or to distant vantage points. When we gather and store information, feelings are elicited and stored also. A broad background whether from real or imagined experiences enables us to learn new concepts.

Preparation: Treasure Chest

Warm-up. *"With your bodies you can move very slowly while keeping your feet in one place.... Now from a seated position, and bending down from the waist, slowly move from your waist up like opening a treasure chest.... Think where you are.... How long has it been since you were last opened?"*

Cool-down. *"Now, close slowly, slowly.... Move your body calmly to a seated position."*

Directed Activity 1:

Show a picture (magazine commercial, art prints, child's drawing, etc.) for stimulation of ideas. Tell the children that they will work in groups to form an interpretation of the picture, first silently with pantomime, and then with sounds and dialogue.

Divide class into groups of six. Remind children that they may be animate and inanimate objects. Circulate to see that all are participating.

Allow forty seconds. *"All group pictures get posed.... Now silently show what is happening.... Now add sound... and, now quietly sit with your group."*

Discussion:

1. *"What was it like being in your group's picture?"*

2. *"What could have been different in your group?"*

Creative Drama

Directed Activity 2:

Direct groups to bring their pictures to life again, this time with each member carrying on dialogue (e.g., grass with the horse, rock with the river, tin can with cat food, etc.) Allow one minute. Half of the group present their "pictures" as others serve as the audience; then reverse.

Discussion:

1. *"What did you do differently in your group this time?"*
2. *"What groups showed humor, sadness, fear, happiness, etc.?"*
3. *"How does playing the part of an animal help you to understand its living conditions?"*
4. *"How do you think your group's situation began?"*
5. *"What have you enjoyed about this activity?"*
6. *"How does sensory awareness increase understanding about objects to which we usually pay no attention?"* (e.g., cause-effect relationship, interdependency, etc.)

Variations:

Social studies pictures "come to life" telling stories of the past.

Science pictures "come to life" explaining scientific concepts.

Math charts, rulers, clocks and graphs "come to life" explaining math concepts.

Summary:

Help the children understand that:

1. Concentration on details and sensory awareness helps a person to gather information.
2. Experiencing through pretending helps a person to learn about concepts.
3. Imagination can facilitate mental travel to microscopic or universal views; and to past, present and future settings.
4. A person's uniqueness is enhanced through the use of imagination, data collection and decision-making.

Uniqueness 6.3
Feelings Graph

Grades: 3-8

Focus:

Range of feelings

Introduction:

A given situation can conjure up a variety of emotions in the people involved. We respond in many different ways depending on what we are doing, our past experiences, and what we want to happen. Emotions hinder or help in learning.... "I am responsible for the feelings I choose to keep...."

Preparation: Loose Arm Machine

Warm-up. "Bend at the waist; let your arms drop gently, keep your feet still and twist from your waist while in bending position. Add a b-z-z-z-z-z or other sound to add machine-like effect."

Cool-down. "Now, become a silent machine that folds up into a little ball on the floor... and now sit in a regular position."

Directed Activity:

Divide into five groups according to the colors the students are wearing. (The object is to have unequal numbers to form a bar graph.)

Red represents angry feelings.
Yellow represents happy, calm feelings.
Green represents energetic, enthusiastic feelings.
Blue represents sad feelings.
Pink represents fearful feelings.

Direct groups to show the feelings they represent with their body movements and voices. Then identify where each row is to be to make a human bar graph of feelings; line up each group. Each row, one at a time, shows its specific "feeling" with sound effects and body movements or gestures.

Have a child go to the board to draw the graph depicted by the rows of children. Discuss "greater than," "less than" and comparison concepts.

Creative Drama

Discussion:

1. *"How did you feel showing the emotion of your group?"*

2. *"Can you automatically feel a certain way when you are assigned an emotion? Why? Why not?"* (Pretending can help understand an emotion that may not be felt.)

3. *"When someone is angry or fearful, what can be done to change that feeling?"* (talk about feeling; draw; tear paper, write; do physical exercises; replace with good feeling from a memory)

4. *"How were the rows different? Alike?"*

5. *"What would it be like if most people in a class were angry? Fearful? Sad?"*

6. *"Which type of feelings allow the most learning?"*

7. *"Which type of feelings in the students are most helpful to a teacher? Parent?"*

Variations:

Graphs show various hobbies.

Graphs show sports, interests, favorite foods.

Summary:

Help the children understand that:

1. In a class many feelings may be present.

2. Some emotions are more helpful in the learning environment than others.

3. Negative feelings can be changed if positive actions and thoughts are taken.

4. People bring into a classroom emotions from past experiences including current emotions.

Uniqueness 6.4

Spotlight

Grades: K-8

Focus:

Self-confidence, eye contact

Introduction:

A way that we know we have value is when people tell us good things about ourselves and the products we produce. As we grow, the goal is to internalize positive messages of self-worth. When we feel worthy and valued, we can better accomplish many tasks.

Preparation: Waking up!

Warm-up. *"We are asleep when suddenly an alarm clock goes off and awakens us. Think how our bodies begin working fast inside when we respond to a loud noise.... Now we are awake but still drowsy...we smell bacon frying... and soon we become alert to begin the day."*

Cool-down. *"Now, our bodies are calming for a night's rest.... Slowly stretch.... Relax... and be ready to rest."*

Directed Activity:

Direct the class to sit in a circle and imagine that a spotlight is turning in the center of the circle. (The facilitator may represent spotlight rays with outstretched arms.) When the light focuses on a person, that person makes a sound or movement spontaneously.

Explain the game of "spotlight." Each person will have a chance to be the "star." The "star" stands while audience members compliment the "star's" inner qualities, attitude, skills or ideas. (Appearance is not included.) The audience member calls the "star" by name, looks at the "star" directly, and compliments.

The "star" responds by looking at the audience member and replying, "Thank you, Sue." The audience member says, "You are welcome." (As time allows there may be compliments from two or three people.)

The facilitator is the last to have a turn complimenting. (This provides an opportunity for children to hear the facilitator's recognition of a child's positive qualities.)

When the "star" sits down, the class applauds.

Discussion:

1. *"How did you feel when you were given nice compliments?"* (We are encouraged when we are genuinely complimented.)

2. *"How does it help you to give a compliment to someone else?"*

3. *"What did you hear about someone else that you would like to have said about you? How can you work toward that?"*

4. *"How often do you like good things said about you?"* (We all need much positive reinforcement several times a day!)

Variations:

Spotlight can be done in small groups so that more compliments are heard for each "star."

Facilitator writes down what the children say and gives it to the "star."

Audience writes "I like you...." notes to each other.

Summary:

Help the children understand that:

1. Genuine compliments help a person internalize positive messages that produce healthy self-esteem.

2. Recognition through verbal or written words, applause, and inclusion in a group build esteem.

3. Positive messages encourage a person to work toward personal goals.

4. Positive communication given orally strengthens the speaker's confidence in public speaking.

5. For competent work, a person needs many positive messages daily.

Uniqueness 6.5

Stepping Stones

Grades: K-8

Focus:

Deficit, compensation, concentration, sensory awareness, understanding others

Introduction:

We all have our strengths and our weaknesses. When we try to overcome a weakness, it is called compensation. In compensating, we enhance our strengths; we "turn stumbling blocks into stepping stones."

Preparation: Butterfly Catching

Warm-up. "We are outside on a beautiful spring day.... Butterflies are everywhere.... We have nets on long poles.... We gently catch one to look at its beauty.... Think what it looks like."

Cool-down. "You are still looking at your butterfly.... Now you are letting it fly away as you gently release it from the net... up it goes; and now sit quietly."

Directed Activity 1:

Explain that people react to situations in different ways; what is hard for one to do may be easy for another. *"Body functions may cause a difficulty which a person struggles with; it can become a building block for skills and understanding if the person has encouragement, determination and the help that is needed."*

Direct the class to form a circle; pretend to be blind by closing your eyes; and then follow directions without looking. *"Standing in your place, copy the sounds I make...."* (hum, whistle, etc.) *"Now, do what I do with your arm...."* (obviously, children do not know what is being done).... *"Now, imagine that you are in a warm pool.... Now follow my hand signal.... Now sit quietly."*

Discussion:

1. *"How did you feel when you were 'blind'?"*

2. *"What could you do well? Not do well?"*

3. *"How did your senses and power of imagination help you?"*

Directed Activity 2:

Help the children to understand that everyone has strengths and weaknesses. *"Compensation is the use of strengths to make up for weaknesses (deficits)."* To help the class understand the frustration of a learning disability, direct several children to the board. *"Write your name with your usual writing hand, and move your opposite foot counter-clockwise."* (Result is that name is scribbled.)

Discussion:

1. *"How does it feel to have difficulty in doing a job?"*
2. *"What are some deficits you have?"*
3. *"How does it feel to be laughed at when you cannot do well?"*
4. *"What thoughtless behaviors occur when a person does not understand another's deficit? How are good sportsmanship and kindness important?"*
5. *"What questions do you have about certain disabilities?"*
6. *"How does a person with a deficit want to be treated?"*
7. *"How does a class or family help a member when there is a problem?*
8. *"How does encouragement build self-confidence?"*
9. *"What laws do you know which help people with severe deficits? How have laws changed over the years?"*

Summary:

Help the children understand that:

1. All people have strengths and weaknesses.
2. Compensation is use of strengths to make up for weaknesses.
3. Encouragement and fair treatment help persons reach for their goals.

Uniqueness 6.6

Tic-Tac-Toe

Grades: 4-8

Focus:

Self-confidence, cooperation, problem solving

Introduction:

We build self-confidence when we express ourselves using voice and body. We help build self-esteem in others when we recognize, encourage and compliment them.

Preparation: High, Low

Warm-up. This may be put to a rhythm or tune and repeated. Use motions. *"Reach up high, then down low, Clap your hands and around you go!"*

Cool-down. Repeat the rhyme ending with "down you go!" indicating to sit quietly.

Directed Activity 1:

A game of tic-tac-toe will be played, using a large grid on the floor made with masking tape. (Each section needs to be large enough for a child to stand.) The class divides in halves, working for the opportunity to put X's and O's on the game board. An X or O goes on the board if all team members participate in role-play. One team member stands on the grid showing the team's symbol by using one's hands and arms. Remind the children that the games are for fun and learning. Good sportsmanship is crucial.

Both teams are given different situations to role-play, showing a positive result using all the team members. They may be animate or inanimate objects. Cooperation and sensitivity to others is important.

Allow forty seconds. (The pace for this activity is fast.) Team X presents while Team O is the audience; then reverse roles. After each presentation, help the class to evaluate if the team incorporated all members in idea-generation and communicated the message. The object is to line up symbols "three in a row." Situations for role-playing:

A person in a wheel-chair is trying to open the door at school. A child is new in school; students laugh at her book bag.

A child is baby-sitting with two younger children; there is a fire in the neighborhood.
A mother asks the children to help buy groceries.
A family is having dinner; a younger child gets ill.
The phone rings and the child is at home alone.
A grandmother is visiting; she cannot hear well.
A friend falls from the swing.
A friend is seen shop-lifting.
A student is seen cheating on a test.
A child does not like to sing at school.
A child is good in art but feels left out at recess.

Discussion:

1. *"What did you like about Team X's story? Why?"*

2. *"What did you like about Team O's story? Why?"*

3. *"Did you feel included in your group? Why? Why not?"*

4. *"How can we have more cooperation in the next stories?"*

Directed Activity 2:

Give the teams new situations. Allow forty seconds. Repeat the process of presenting and discussing. Encourage the team members to compliment other's contributions. Identify the various forms of participation, both verbal and non-verbal.

Discussion:

1. *"What kinds of communication did you see demonstrated?"*

2. *"How was self-confidence displayed?"* (e.g., strong voice, definite body actions, etc.)

3. *"How were problems solved in the presentation?"*

4. *"Who displayed the ability to encourage others?"*

5. *"What compliments can you think of for the opposite team?"*

Variations:

To put X or O on the grid, teams must:

Answer subject content questions.
Role-play positive sayings to encourage others.
Act out scientific concepts.
Demonstrate game skills in physical education.

Summary:

Help the children understand that:

1. Self-confidence is built when a person expresses ideas.
2. Expression of ideas can take many forms.
3. Being included helps a person to want to contribute to group-work.
4. Good sportsmanship helps everyone feel encouraged.

TV Commercial
for a Special Person

Grades: 2-8

Focus:

Awareness of positive qualities, advertisements, persuasion

Introduction:

We can help other people feel good about themselves, and to feel worthy and valuable. When we are being encouragers, we are strengthening our own good qualities. If we feel successful, we are more likely to become successful.

Preparation: Jiggle and Wiggle

Warm-up. Lead with this rhyme as actions are added:

"Jiggle and wiggle; one. two. three;
Jiggle and wiggle; get down on your knee;
Jiggle and wiggle and turn around."

Cool-down. *"Jiggle and wiggle and touch the ground! (or 'sit on the ground')."*

Directed Activity:

The children are seated in a circle. Discuss the purpose of commercials or advertisements. Direct them to raise their arms at shoulder height, bending their arms from the elbow, to become TV screens with their faces becoming the TV announcers. *"Pretend you are giving information on television.... Now give an advertisement about a famous person."* (Beginning with simple topics may be helpful, e.g. dog food, breakfast cereal, etc.)

Direct partners to work together, each planning a commercial to advertise the partner's good qualities. Remind them that when a close look is taken, many good things can be observed about a person; and that commercials persuade using positive qualities to publicize a "product" in a short period of time. After the partners work together for two minutes, two pairs get together for sharing. The four each take turns presenting advertisements. They have one minute each to give an advertisement.

Qualities that may be described are listed:

Friendly, kind courteous
Intelligent, artistic
Good sport, fair, honest
Humorous, fun-loving
Brave, strong, determined
Helpful, encouraging, interesting
Loving, caring, thoughtful
Good worker, industrious, thorough

Discussion:

1. *"What did you like the most about the activity? Why?"*

2. *"How were ads similar? Different?"*

3. *"If you advertised yourself. what are your most outstanding qualities that you would present?"*

4. *"What are some qualities you would like to add to the ones you already have? How could that happen?"*

Variations:

Advertise school subjects.
Advertise your family.
Advertise a group project.

For older groups, study of commercials, the main selling techniques, attention-getting devices, and summary statements may be used.

Groups may use this format to sell a product with two forming a screen, others being the announcer, the product and the people in the ad.

Summary:

Help the children understand that:

1. Every person has unique qualities.

2. Looking for good qualities in others builds a person's understanding of the importance of positive attitude.

3. Complimenting encourages the other person's growth.

4. Sharing positive thoughts builds group spirit.

Chapter VII
Models

Hearts and Heroes, Lesson 7.3

Models

Models 7.1

Family Circle

Grades: K-8

Focus:

Families, roles, love, responsibility, fun, help, respect, strength

Introduction:

Understanding about family roles and functions is increased when we have opportunities to take on different roles of family members.

Preparation: Loose Arm Machine

Warm-up. "Bend at the waist; let your arms drop gently. keep your feet still and twist from your waist while in bending position. Add a b-z-z-z-z-z or other sound to add machine-like effect."

Cool-down. "Now. become a silent machine that folds up into a little ball on the floor... and now sit in a regular position."

Directed Activity 1:

The children sit in groups of six. Lead a discussion about family units, kinds of families, and the different roles in a family. Each group will role-play an assigned family; members may choose their roles. Emphasize that families shall be happy, helpful and caring. Allow three minutes for groups to work; then, one group at a time presents its family while the others serve as the audience. Members not having family roles may be neighbors, friends and so forth. Family-types are assigned:

Two-parent family, four children
Single-parent family, three children
Grandparents in parenting role to two children
Aunt, uncle in parenting role to one child
Friend in parenting role to two children while mother is in hospital; the friend has two children of her own

Discussion:

1. "How did it feel to be in your family?"

2. "What were the clues about people's feelings?"

3. "How are parent roles different from children's roles? Alike?"

4. *"What activities or ways of acting made you feel good? Why?"*

5. *"How do family members contribute to each other's good feelings?"*

6. *"When there are problems, how do caring families solve them?"*

7. *"How do family members help others in these areas?"*

> love
> work
> learning
> sharing
> strength
> responsibility
> respect
> fun, leisure

Directed Activity 2:

Direct the groups to improvise a happy activity in which all members plan, participate or encourage. Allow three minutes for work; then, one group at a time presents its family.

Suggested activities:

> Celebrating a holiday
> Going on a vacation
> Sharing interests
> Spending time together
> Deciding how to spend money on leisure activity

Discussion:

1. *"How did you feel when you heard specific comments?"*

2. *"Did you see a family activity that you would like? What was it?"*

3. *"What, to you, is important in a family?"*

4. *"What do you never want to do in the family that you will have when you grow up?"*

5. *"Why is being responsible so important in a family?"*

6. *"How is cooperation helpful?"*

7. *"How is fun an important part of family life?"*

Variation:

Groups choose a problem to solve by working together with family members.

Summary:

Help the children understand that:

1. Each family member is important and has needs to feel belonging, safety, love and respect.
2. Parents' roles have certain responsibilities which are different from children's roles.
3. Healthy families help all members to be their best.

Models 7.2

Storming for Ideas

Grades: 4-8

Focus:

Brainstorming, respect, creative thinking, communication, self-confidence

Introduction:

Brainstorming is one of the most effective ways for groups to work together in finding creative solutions. The value-free atmosphere builds self-confidence in members while providing opportunity for idea-generation. Fear of failure kills much creativity. Childlike inquisitiveness keeps creative processes alive.

Preparation: Bend and Pick

Warm-up. "Stand, bend from the waist down, now bend at the knees, then back up; each time you are near the ground, look for something you can imagine picking up and putting in your pocket. Stand, bend, and pick." (Repeat three times.)

Cool-down. "Now all your pockets are full, and you move carefully to sit down so nothing in your pockets makes a sound."

Directed Activity 1:

Direct groups of six to show the concept of "idea-explosion" by thinking of ways to demonstrate patriotism by using body movements and voices. Group members compact with each other very closely. At the facilitator's signal, "explosion" occurs and each member individually demonstrates being patriotic by using body movement, sounds and dialogue. Allow thirty seconds for work time. Half the groups watch, half perform. Help the class to observe each idea for showing patriotism. Reverse the process with the second half showing ways to demonstrate caring for the environment.

Discussion:

1. *"How were the groups different? Alike?"*

2. *"What other words or concepts can be shown in an 'explosion'?"*

3. *"Which ideas are correct?"* (None are correct or incorrect in the idea-generation process.)

Directed Activity 2:

Direct the groups to consider the following in the next activity:

Rules for Brainstorming

1. Define the subject or problem to be brainstormed. (All involved in the group need to understand the problem they are trying to solve.)

2. Write down all the ideas where everyone can see. (Words, phrases, or symbols stimulate new ideas and relationships.)

3. No "no-no's." (The goal is ideas, not judgments. Accept all ideas, even non-sensible ones.)

4. Hitchhike. (Pick up on another's idea and ride with it to trigger more ideas.)

5. Concentrate on quantity and speed.

6. Keep it loose. (Keep comments like,"That's good!" or "How stupid!" out of the process.)

Brainstorm the following situation: making new students in school feel welcome. One group member serves as a recorder, writing ideas on a large sheet of paper or board while everyone contributes for one minute. Then, direct the groups to choose three to five of their ideas to show through characterization and dialogue. Allow two minutes for group work. Each group presents its activity while the others serve as the audience.

Discussion:

1. *"In the brainstorming time. did you feel that you were part of the group?"*

2. *"How does working together help in getting more ideas?"*

3. *"What rules were difficult to follow?"*

4. *"How would you have felt if your ideas were ridiculed? What would have happened?"*

5. *"How do the rules encourage self-confidence? Creativity?"* (no judgment, any idea is okay, everyone contributes, no one is boss, etc.)

6. *"What have you learned in this activity that is important to you?"*

Variations:

Groups quickly brainstorm a situation writing down ideas, then explore ideas in these ways:

Each member pantomimes a different idea.
Pairs show an idea.
The group combines several ideas and demonstrates through fantasy or fictitious characters.

Guidance-oriented topics could include these:

Getting homework done
Making and keeping friends
Asking for help
Dealing with siblings
Caring for neighbor's pets
Handling problems

Summary:

Help the children understand that:

1. Brainstorming is a creative way to stimulate new ideas in a value-free climate.

2. Childlike inquisitiveness promotes creative thinking.

3. Creative thinking promotes self-confidence.

4. Group cooperation fosters a positive climate for personal growth.

Models 7.3

Hearts and Heroes

Grades: K-8

Focus:

Positive qualities, American democratic values, family, friends, famous people, dialogue

Introduction:

Practicing the behaviors of famous leaders who exemplify positive qualities enables us to develop personal patterns for current and future actions.

Preparation: Time Machine

Warm-up. "Stand; get inside the time machine.... You have to fill it up completely by expanding yourself as much as you can."

Cool-down. "Now, decrease in size and become microscopic as you sit on the floor."

Directed Activity 1:

Lead a discussion about qualities liked in others, (e.g., courtesy, helpfulness, courage, honesty, integrity, etc.). Children work in groups of six and enact positive qualities in problem situations. Allow three minutes for group work. Half of the groups present their improvisations simultaneously while the others serve as the audience; then repeat with groups reversing roles of players and audience. Problem situations are assigned:

> Money is stolen
> Child is lost in a store
> Cheating was done on a test
> You are falsely accused of causing a rumor
> Angry customer steps in front of you in cash register line

Discussion:

1. "What qualities were portrayed that you would like to see in your family? What qualities would you like to see in your friends?"
2. "Which qualities do you usually show to others?"

Directed Activity 2:

This activity calls for background information about famous persons. It may be taught by the teacher, related by

Creative Drama

"researchers" in groups, or read by all participants before the activity. The name of a famous person, personal data, accomplishments, and period of history can be written on index cards for a quick review, if the class has already learned about the persons. Direct each child to show the positive qualities of a famous leader to the group. Use voice and movement to show qualities of a person in this list:

George Washington: honest, leader
Benjamin Franklin: creative, industrious, patriotic
Pocahontas: caring, brave
Amelia Earhart: adventurous, brave
Abraham Lincoln: gentle, persuasive
Will Rogers: humorous, creative
Helen Keller: persistent, resourceful
Louis Pasteur: curious, diligent
Susan B. Anthony: determined
Jonas Salk: studious, problem-solver
Martin L. King: visionary, committed
Sally Ride: curious, determined
Sam Houston: courageous, daring, determined
Thomas Edison: inventive, compensator (he never learned to read)

Discussion:

1. *"In what ways were similar qualities shown by different people?"*

2. *"What qualities did you enact or see in other characters for which you would like to be known?"*

3. *"How does learning about famous people help us?"*

Summary:

Help the children understand that:

1. Positive qualities that build encouragement and faith contribute to leadership.

2. A good leader encourages growth in self and others.

3. A good leader looks for ways to get problems solved by working with others.

4. A good leader has ideals that benefit self and others; and sets goals.

5. What is modeled as a youth may be a pattern for future behavior.

Models 7.4

What Do You Do?

Grades: K-8

Focus:

Personal traits, recall

Introduction:

Positive qualities in people we admire can become models for our own behaviors. Thinking how a special person would put positive qualities into action can be a pattern for our choices.

Preparation: Waking from Hibernation

Warm-up. *"With our arms close to us and sitting on the floor, let us bend as though we were cold and asleep. Now it is getting to be springtime, and we are animals coming out of hibernation.... Think what animal you are.... Add sounds at a low volume."*

Cool-down. *"Now we are outside stretching silently in the sunlight. Slowly stretch and calm yourself now for a long nap."*

Directed Activity:

Tell the children that they will work together, but use their own ideas in this activity. Ask the students to think of a special person they have liked. What behavior or inner qualities of that person would they want to model? Identify positive versus negative qualities. Honesty, friendliness, kindness and understanding may be named. Direct the children to enact these special qualities in the following situations.

"A new student has just come into the class; what do you do?"

"Two students get into a fight on the playground; what do you, as a responsible person, do?"

"Your mom has told you that you cannot go into someone else's house unless an adult is there. An adult is not at your friend's house, and your friend wants you to come inside to play. The statement made is, 'I will not be your friend if you do not come inside and play with me!' What do you do?"

"Your friend wants you to smoke a cigarette. You do not want to. Statements are made like, 'You're scared!', 'You can't do anything wrong,' 'You're a chicken!' What do you do?"

Discussion:

1. *"How did you feel when you played the part of your special person?"*

2. *"How does thinking of a special person's good quality help you act positively?"*

3. *"When a negative interaction begins, what can you do to change it?"*

4. *"What do you know about health and safety that would be good to recall?"*

5. *"What have you learned today that will help you in making decisions later?"*

6. *"What are some ways of behaving that you are not going to use?"*

Variation:

Role-play situations, thinking of positive qualities in family members to serve as models.

Summary:

Help the children understand that:

1. Behavior is often modeled from what is seen in others.

2. Remembering positive models of behavior helps in choosing to act in certain ways.

Models 7.5

Speaker's Spot

Grades: 4-8

Focus:

Oral communication, narration, self-confidence, audience skills

Introduction:

After practicing speaking and receiving encouragement, we are willing to try again and to risk even more. Standing in front of an audience and speaking becomes easier.

Preparation: Sounds All Around

Warm-up. "Stand very still. Listen to sounds all around. Pick out one to pantomime." (Example: car outside—student pretends to be driving; pencil sharpener—student pretends to be using sharpener.) "Each person, stay in your place and show what you hear, then add sounds."

Cool-down. "Now, pretend all sounds stop, and as you sit, think of silence."

Directed Activity 1:

Divide the class into groups of six. An imaginary "Speaker's Spot" is designated in each group's circle where the "speaker" stands. One member in each group is the "speaker." The "speaker" tells a story while the other members pantomime the narration. Remind the children that animate and inanimate objects may be characterized, and that one child may enact more than one role. Allow one minute for group work.

As a group presents its improvisation, others serve as audience members, applauding at proper times. The "speaker" is encouraged to use various inflections and sound effects to add to the mood of the story. These are ideas for improvisations:

Family's dog was lost and has come home
Neighbor's cat has new kittens
Class went to the zoo
Family went to the rodeo
Little boy is having his tonsils out
Girl did not keep up with the time, and she is an hour late getting home

Discussion:

1. *"How did you feel being in your group? Why?"*
2. *"How did the speaker help the audience to understand the story?"*
3. *"How is oral communication different from communication with body movements or gestures?"*
4. *"How were the plots of the groups similar? Different?"*
5. *"What jobs or careers involve much oral communication with groups?"*
6. *"Which groups showed animate objects? Inanimate?"*
7. *"As speakers, how did you feel? Why?"*
8. *"As actors, how did you feel? Why?"*
9. *"As audience members, what were your responsibilities?"*

Summary:

Help the children understand that:

1. Speaking in front of a group builds self-confidence.
2. Accurate communication of facts and ideas builds understanding.
3. Appropriate audience responses show appreciation and build confidence in the presenters.

Models 7.6

The Student's Role

Grades: K-8

Focus:

Roles, characterization, appropriate behavior

Introduction:

When we understand the roles that are appropriate in specific settings, we are more able to be participants and contributors to the group process and learning.

Preparation: Forest and Giants

Warm-up. Walking in a circle say, *"We are going through a big forest. The trees tower over us; hear the cracking leaves under our feet.... Now. we shall become giants. and look out over the tree-tops as we continue around."*

Cool-down. *"Now. as sleepy giants. we walk slowly and become heavier and heavier... until we find a resting place."* Signal to get in a seated position.

Directed Activity:

Direct the class to pantomime being a player on a football team. Ask what would happen if during a football game a player began trying to shoot a basket as in basketball; responses can lead into the idea that when a role is to be filled, it has particular jobs within it that are to be done, and certain things are not to be done. (e.g., A football player does not lead cheers or play an instrument during the game.) *"We perform different roles depending upon who we are with. where we are. and the activity involved. A student has a special role of proper ways to be and act."*

Divide the children into groups of six to characterize appropriate and inappropriate behavior of students in a classroom. Someone may play the teacher's role. Allow three minutes for improvisation; circulate to observe which roles children take, encourage all to take specific behaviors.

Appropriate:
Comes to school on time, prepared
Greets others
Listens to the teacher
Follows class rules
Starts work on time
Uses time wisely
Knows how to ask for help
Acts appropriately with others

Inappropriate:
Comes to school late, unprepared
Ignores others
Does not listen to the teacher
Ignores class rules
Slow to start work
Poor use of time
Does not try to get help
Acts inappropriately with others

Discussion:

1. *"How did you feel playing the role you had?"*

2. *"What appropriate roles do you play in the regular classroom?"*

3. *"How do you feel when someone takes the role of class-clown. gossiper. or boss?"*

4. *"What kinds of actions (behaviors) help you learn? How?"*

5. *"What behaviors disrupt learning? How?"*

6. *"How is this going to help you to be a better student?"*

7. *"How can you encourage friends to have better behaviors?"*

8. *"Why are rules and laws established?"*

8. *"What civic values are reflected in school rules?"*

Variations:

Enact appropriate and inappropriate behaviors of theatre audience members.

Enact appropriate behaviors for roles played in family (e.g., as helper, as pet care-giver, as brother or sister, etc.)

Summary:

Help the children understand that:

1. The student role has expectations that are consistent.

2. Students learn better when they fulfill the student role effectively.

3. Appropriate behavior helps a person to be more likable than inappropriate behavior.

Models 7.7

We Are Problem Solvers

Grades: 4-8

Focus:

Problem solving, choices, actions, thoughts

Introduction:

When the problem solving model for decision making is studied, practiced and understood, we feel more secure and effective.

Preparation: Push the Walls Away

Warm-up. "Stand; take two deep breaths; now 'push' the walls away, relax; now 'push the ceiling up,' relax." (Repeat once using sounds to show exertion.)

Cool-down. "Your arms need to rest; let them quietly pull your body weight down to a sitting position."

Directed Activity:

The class is divided with half being actors and half being audience. Direct the actors to form an outline of stair steps that lead to a door at the top. Tell the students that each step represents a step in the problem-solving process. One person volunteers to work on a problem and walk up the steps as the audience members share ideas in solving the problem. Example: The problem is that the student has a "left-out" feeling on the school playground.

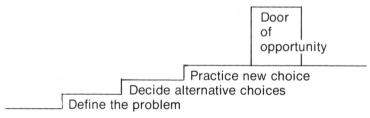

Step 1: Define the problem. What is wrong? What do I want to happen so this will no longer remain a problem?

The child defines the problem; a group of five from the audience may role-play a situation in which a child is left out. The audience helps define actions which caused the problem.

Step 2: Decide what needs to be done. What are the alternatives? What can I choose to do or to feel?

The child decides and demonstrates what kinds of actions and thoughts to take. The audience helps by giving positive messages and suggestions:

"I will act friendly."
"I will talk with people."
"I will ask someone to join or help me."

Step 3: Practice new choices of actions and feelings.

The child practices what will be done to solve the problem. The audience encourages by clapping.

Open the Door! *"I am ready for a new opportunity."*

The child pretends to open the door to a new opportunity by using new choices to solve the problem.

Discussion:

1. *"Do we all view problems the same way? What causes us to see them differently?"*

2. *"How can talking about a problem be helpful?"*

3. *"How do new ideas help in problem-solving?"*

4. *"What are other problems we can work through?"*

Summary:

Help the children understand that:

1. A problem may lead to new understanding.

2. Working to solve a problem gives a person a sense of power and pride.

Chapter VIII
Processes

Clutter Bug, Lesson 8.2

Processes 8.1

The Human Body Machine

Grades: K-8

Focus:

Interdependency, cause and effect, health practices

Introduction:

Body parts and functions are interrelated. Each mechanism has a specific job. When one part is influenced by external or internal factors, other parts may be influenced also.

Preparation: Frowns and Clowns

Warm-up. "*Our faces, bodies, and voices tell our feelings. First, let us look very sad... now, happy.... Silently be a clown with definite movements as we go around in a circle.*"

Cool-down. "Now, calmly be a clown in slow motion... and go back to your space very quietly."

Directed Activity:

Depending on size and grade of the class, decide which body parts will be portrayed, (e.g., brain, heart, lungs, stomach, eyes, nose, mouth, ears, arms, legs). Children are assigned or decide which body part to enact with movement and sound. They get in positions and act out their body-part functions as the narration occurs.

"*As healthy things happen, body parts work in unison; as unhealthy habits take over, parts have more difficulty doing their jobs. Show that you are working harder.... You are having more trouble doing your job.... You are slowing down.... Now the body is resting and regaining energy.*"

Additional suggestions may be used:

The alarm clock rings.... The body begins moving. (walking, movement)
The body is riding a bicycle. (exercise)
Now it takes in an egg, milk, orange juice, and toast. (sensory functions, nutrition)

Creative Drama

The body is at a desk at school. (attention, focus)
Now it is having an unexpected test. (feeling of fear)
Now it is responding to a friend's compliment. (feeling of belonging)

Discussion:

1. *"How did you feel as the part you played? What was your job?"*

2. *"How did you feel when you experienced the unhealthy habit?"*

3. *"How did you work with others?"*

4. *"What important things have you learned about keeping your body healthy?"*

Variations:

Class demonstrates a cell, its structure, and function.

Groups show dental hygiene by portraying teeth, gum, plaque, and tooth brushing.

Children demonstrate circulatory, respiratory and digestive processes.

Summary:

Help the children understand that:

1. Good health habits help a whole body to function well.

2. Improper health habits may cause body systems to become less effective and less efficient.

3. Body parts work separately and in cooperation with other parts.

Processes 8.2

Clutter Bug

Grades: K-8

Focus:

Organization, study skills, cleanliness

Introduction:

Having a sense of organization in dealing with objects and ideas allows us to effectively work, play and rest. Not all people have the same ability to organize. Organizational skills can be learned.

Preparation: Hopping

Warm-up. *"Stand, get ready to hop around the circle. Think of all kinds of things that hop, and as we begin, pretend to be one of those things."*

Cool-down. End with the signal to "freeze," then in slow motion "float" down to a seated position.

Directed Activity:

Divide the class into halves. The children represent different items within a messy desk; each decides what to be (e.g., crayon, gum, paper, tissues). Each group designates one student to be the one who clutters. Allow thirty seconds for the groups to personify their objects and to interact with the other objects in the desk. One group at a time presents its "cluttered situation" to others who serve as the audience. Then the "student" unclutters the contents as the "desk items" help by cooperating and moving where they are placed.

Discussion:

1. *"How did you feel inside the cluttered desk?"*
2. *"How was it a different feeling when the desk was organized?"*
3. *"How did the desk look before cleaning and afterwards?"*
4. *"What, in your own world, is cluttered? How can it become more organized?"*

Creative Drama

5. *"How does organization help within a family?"*

6. *"How do we use organization in other ways at school?"* (e.g., papers, lockers, room arrangement, thinking through homework, reading and recalling information.)

7. *"Why is organized thinking important to a scientist?"* (steps of the scientific process)

8. *"How have astronauts, historians, lawyers used organizational skills?"*

9. *"How do we organize thoughts in working a math problem?"*

Variations:

Organize homework materials to take home.

Organize thoughts and ideas for a story.

Organize and review math concepts needed for an assignment.

Summary:

Help the children understand that:

1. Organization helps in all areas of living.

2. Skills of organization can be learned by practicing.

3. Responsibility for personal and public property involves organized actions and thinking.

From a Different Point of View

Grades: K-8

Focus:

Viewpoints, feelings, responsibility, conflict, environment

Introduction:

A situation that is a problem to one person may not be seen the same way by another person. Different viewpoints can lead to conflict. Understanding a person's ideas from one's point of view helps to better understand the other person's actions and feelings.

Preparation: Flowers Opening

Warm-up. "*With our arms close to our bodies, kneeling down on the floor in a small ball, let us begin slowly growing like flowers.... Heads slowly up.... Arms as leaves.... Now we are fully grown and the wind is blowing.... Sway in the breeze.*"

Cool-down. "*Now it is calm again.... Slowly calm your body movements as evening comes across the sky.*"

Directed Activity 1:

The children stand in a circle. Using interpretative movements and sounds, they portray forest plants, large and small; vegetable plants in a garden.

Discussion:

1. "*What type of plant are you?*"

2. "*What does a lady bug look like to you? A human being?*"

3. "*If a giant came along, how would you appear to the giant?*"

Directed Activity 2:

Direct groups of six to work for two minutes, and then one group at a time presents their ideas while the others serve as the audience. Use characterization and dialogue to show a problem, then resolution of conflict in these situations:

A flower bed with many kinds of plants
A flower bed and an allergic family member
A flower bed and an invalid elderly neighbor
A flower bed and a rowdy group of children

Discussion:

1. *"What did you do that you liked?"*

2. *"What was the conflict in your situation? How was it solved?"*

3. *"How was the flower bed seen differently in the different groups?"*

4. *"What made differences in the way people reacted?"*

5. *"Suppose a happy gardener saw children walking in the flower bed. How would the gardener feel? What might happen?"*

6. *"How does being tired or ill affect a person's outlook?"*

Variations:

Other situations can be explored:

Parents divorcing
Vast population in a country growing
Cutting down timber in a forest
Shopping mall built near neighborhood

Summary:

Help the children understand that:

1. A different point of view can lead to understanding when there has been conflict.

2. Trying to see a problem from a larger perspective can produce new insights.

3. Empathy helps to understand another person's problems.

Garden Competition

Grades: K-8

Focus:

Interrelatedness in environment, cultivated and wild plants, natural cycles, weather, climate, regions, environmental hazards

Introduction:

Man and environment are interdependent. The more we understand interrelationships of cause and effect, the greater our awareness of the need to be care takers of our environment and our bodies.

Preparation: Melting Ice Cream

Warm-up. "*Standing, reach up high, then low. Now, pretend to be ice cream on a warm, windy day. Make a sound to show what is happening.*"

Cool-down. End with the signal to "freeze," then slowly drop your body to a seated position as a humming sound is made. When seated, sounds stop.

Directed Activity 1:

Direct the students to pretend to be seeds planted or scattered on the soil. *"Think what type of seed you are"* (e.g., pea, blue-bonnet, tomato, grass, cotton, morning-glory). *"Decide where you are growing"* (e.g., forest, desert, hill, garden, river bank). *"With body movements in your space, you begin to grow. You have to push hard to grow.... Think about the soil and the climate where you are.... Now you are in the sunlight and it is springtime. It begins to rain.... Think how this affects you depending on where you are located. Now, the season is changing; it is summer.... There is less rain in your area than usual.... What happens to you? Fall is coming.... How do you look now?... Winter comes. How does the cold weather affect you?"*

Creative Drama

Discussion:

1. *"What type of plant were you?"* (Point out the differences between cultivated and wild plants.)

2. *"How did you feel as you began to grow?"*

3. *"When did you feel the best? The worst?"*

4. *"What were some troubles?"*

Directed Activity 2:

Lead in playing out some events which could promote or hinder growth. Direct the children to respond as plants in these situations:

A developer builds commercial buildings
Flowers are picked for a bouquet
A bird scratches for seeds
Pesticides are sprayed
There is a lack of water
Floods come
A new highway is constructed
Bike riders run over plants

Discussion:

1. *"How did you feel when some of those things happened to you?"*

2. *"What do wild plants and cultivated plants have in common?"*

3. *"How could concerned people have helped you?"*

4. *"How do personal view-points result in different uses of plants in the natural environment?"*

Summary:

Help the children understand that:

1. Man and nature are interdependent; man's actions upon the environment create reactions which eventually affect man.

2. Natural factors as winds, floods and climate affect the various life cycles.

Processes 8.5

Guitar, Singer, Conductor

Grades: 4-8

Focus:

Change in roles, conflict, resolution, acceptance

Introduction:

When change occurs, roles, boundaries and communication systems become unbalanced until new functions are identified. When we understand change and its results, we deal with negative feelings better.

Preparation: Humming Twist

Warm-up. "Standing, twist slowly from your waist up; keep moving your shoulders, head, and eyes as far as you can go. Now, to the opposite side. Repeat three times. Make humming sounds going from side to side."

Cool-down. End with the signal to "freeze," then slowly drop your body to a seated position as a humming sound is made. When seated, sounds, stop.

Directed Activity 1:

Direct the class to pantomime playing or being musical instruments: stringed, wind or percussion. Then pantomime singing and conducting. Divide the class into groups of six. Each decides to be an instrument or singer. Work together for one minute, thinking of a particular song or piece of music to perform. Half of the group present their idea while the others are the audience; reverse player and audience roles.

Discussion:

1. "What do you like about your group?"

2. "How are you a part of your group?"

3. "What could be different in you group?"

Creative Drama

Directed Activity 2:

Direct groups to portray some of these ideas after three minutes of group work. Half of the group present while others are the audience.

The facilitator plays the role of a new singer who says, "I've come to take your place!" What happens?

Someone new comes in and gets to play a solo on an instrument. What happens?

The conductor changes the method of directing (from outgoing to shy; boisterous to orderly; classical to jazz). What happens?

Discussion:

1. *"What part did you like doing the most? What made you most uncomfortable?"*
2. *"How does this remind you of feelings you may have had?"*
3. *"What was the conflict? How was that problem solved? What could be some other choices?"*

Variations:

A substitute teacher is in charge of the class.

A new student comes into class; this student is very good in sports.

A classmate moves; you do not have a close friend.

Family rules are changed about cleaning duties; use of money.

Summary:

Help the children understand that:

1. When change occurs, every person in the group is affected.
2. Understanding that conflict and negativism often come with change helps prepare a person to deal with one's feelings.
3. Changes in friendships, work groups, authority and family produce many kinds of feelings.

Processes 8.6

Range of Feelings

Grades: K-8

Focus:

Feelings, sensitivity to others, continuum

Introduction:

The continuum concept helps children learn there is a wide range of feelings that can be attached to any past, present or future experience. Feelings are never "right" or "wrong"; behaviors may be addressed as acceptable or unacceptable, but the feelings which precede and result from behaviors are real and valid.

Preparation: Jiggle and Wiggle

Warm-up. Lead with this rhyme as actions are added:
"Jiggle and wiggle; one, two, three;
Jiggle and wiggle; get down on your knee;
Jiggle and wiggle and turn around."

Cool-down. *"Jiggle and wiggle and touch the ground! (or 'sit on the ground')."*

Directed Activity 1:

Direct the children to form a line segment. *"The two persons at the ends show two points, but everyone else is also a point on the line segment. If we called the end at the left 'all the time' and the other end 'never,' we could ask a question like 'When do you like to swim?' and answers from a group would be at different locations."*

Example:

All the time	Never

Have two children place themselves on the continuum in regard to answers about swimming.

Discussion:

1. *"Which child is right?"* (Of course, there is not a right or wrong answer to this! Feelings, likes and dislikes can be similar or dissimilar to other people's.)

Creative Drama

2. *"What could happen for one of these persons to change one's feelings?"* (weather effects, favorite friend invites you to a movie, accident produces fear.)

Directed Activity 2:

Have the class sit as the audience. Direct four children to be ready to stand as a new continuum, two additional children at the ends being "excited" and "worried." This is the problem: *"Your class is going on a bus to the park for a picnic."* Have the four place themselves on the continuum to show their feelings.

Discussion (directed to children on the line):

1. *"Why did you place yourself in that position? Who were you most like in your feelings?*

2. *"What might be some things that would make a person worry about the picnic?"* (gets car-sick, does not have a lunch to take, is afraid of bus.)

3. *"If a person is scared of something, how does it help to distinguish between a fear based on fact or a fear based on fantasy?"*

4. *"What might be okay for one person might bother another. Can you think of an example?"*

Directed Activity 3:

Set up two more continuums so that all children may participate. Use a situation as this: *"Your report card had A's and B's. How do you feel...? Pleased? Disappointed?"* (continuum extremes)

Discussion:

1. *"Who has feelings that are in a close range? Far apart?"* (Compare by looking at all groups.)

2. *"When we realize that a friend is at the worried point, or seems to be having trouble or fear, what can we do to help? What type of help can the person get?"*

Variations:

Continuum activities can be based on these examples:

The family pet disappears. How do you feel? Why?

_____

sad   happy

Mother is happy about quitting her job. How do you feel? Why?

_____
happy   sad

You and Dad are going to spend the whole Saturday together. How do you feel?

_____
worried   excited

You decide whether to have a nutritious or junk food snack.

_____
wise   unwise

Summary:

Help the children understand that:

1. All feelings are real; they may be based on reality or unreality, but the feelings are important parts of attitude.

2. People have many feelings; they cover a broad range from negative to positive extremes.

3. There are many degrees of feelings.

4. A person may change feelings about a situation without the situation itself changing.

5. A situation may change, producing a change in a person's feelings.

Choices to Stay Healthy

Grades: 4-8

Focus:

Body functions, cause-effect, health practices, laws, decision-making, peer pressure, substance abuse

Introduction:

Decisions that lead to health help persons to feel in control of themselves. To face difficult decisions, it helps to have the opportunity to rehearse responses; "practice without pressure" leads to wiser decisions in real-life situations.

Preparation: Melting Ice Cream

Warm-up. *"Standing, reach up high, then low. Now, pretend to be ice cream on a warm, windy day. Make a sound to show what is happening."*

Cool-down. End with the signal to "freeze," then slowly drop your body to a seated position as a humming sound is made. When seated, sounds stop.

Directed Activity 1:

Some teaching about effects of certain chemicals in the body will need to be done before this activity. Each person is a body part; some may work together to form the brain, the lungs and so forth. Narrate the following activities as students respond with body movements and sound effects:

"You are a healthy body; do your specific job using motion and sounds.... Now the body is getting very tired; show what happens to you.... Now the body is taking in alcohol (liver and brain especially affected). *The body is taking in cigarette smoke; now it is taking in marijuana smoke."* (THC in marijuana clings to fatty tissues in brain and liver). Point out multiple health and safety problems caused by substance abuse if children don't clearly demonstrate them.

Discussion:

(Questions can be posed after each specific activity listed above.)

1. *"How did your body feel?*
2. *"What did you want to happen?"*
3. *"What were some of the interactions between the different body parts?"*
4. *"What words describe the body when it has trouble?"* (exhaustion, illness, frustration)

Directed Activity 2:

Divide the class into groups of six. *"We shall be role-playing situations where a person wants you to try smoking, etc. Your job is to keep your whole body healthy by the decisions you make and your assertive communication. In your group practice what you will say and do when the facilitator challenges you."* Only the facilitator takes the challenger role; this technique helps to monitor more closely and control negative interactions. Help the children to think of and try out assertive behaviors to reject negative influences by saying "no," having reasons for positive choices, using humor, etc. Help the children to understand that in dangerous situations, they must quickly decide if something is harmful, illegal or unacceptable; if so, a quick "no," getting away and getting help from an adult is imperative.

One group at a time is challenged; the other groups serve as the audience. As the challenger, the facilitator tries to get students to:

Smoke cigarettes
Drink alcoholic beverages
Take unprescribed medicines
Sniff glue or paint
Smoke marijuana
Mix "uppers" and "downers"
Join in trying to convince others to participate in drug abuse

Discussion:

1. *"How did you feel when you were challenged?"*
2. *"How did you feel when you answered?"*

3. *"How did working through a problem-situation before it happened help you?"*

4. *"How do laws help keep us healthy and safe?"* (e.g., age limits, prescriptions, etc.)

Summary:

Help the children understand that:

1. Body parts and functions are interrelated.

2. A change in one function produces other changes.

3. It is important to understand how to make decisions leading to health.

4. Persons feel in control of themselves when they think about a possible problem situation and how they would respond before it happens.

Creative Drama

Bibliography

Axline, V. (1947). *Play therapy.* New York: Ballantine Books.

Play therapy is a vital opportunity that is given to children to "play out" their feelings and problems -their fears, hatred, loneliness and feelings of failure and inadequacy. This book is an important and rewarding resource for parents, teachers -anyone who comes in contact with children.

Bank, S.P. & Kahn, M.D. (1982). *The sibling bond.* New York: Basic Books, Inc.

This is a major account of the powerful emotional connections among brothers and sisters throughout life.

Bean, R. & Clemes, H. (1980). *How to raise children's self-esteem, How to discipline children without feeling guilty, How to teach children responsibility,* and *How to raise teenagers' self-esteem.* San Jose, CA: Enrich, Div./Ohaus.

Bloch, D. (1978). *So the witch won't eat me.* Boston: Houghton Mifflin Company.

The author, who is a psychologist and a psychoanalyst, explores fantasy and the child's fear of infanticide, the fantasy of the devalued self and anticipation of punishment. Pointing out that ways to control these fears are usually self deception and defensive measures, the author shares how treatment can be effective in resolving emotional problems.

Bos, B. (1983). *Before the basics: Creating conversations with children.* Sacramento, CA: Cal Central Press.

The author of this book extends examples of language, music and movement activities which provide pre-reading language experiences. This book can be used by parents and teachers alike who want to make learning an active participatory experience.

Briggs, D.C. (1970). *Your child's self-esteem.* Garden City, NY: Doubleday.

This book focuses on the child's self-esteem, its importance in relation to health, its antecedents, and methods parents can use to foster self-esteem.

Canfield, J. & Wells, H.C. (1976). *100 ways to enhance self-concept in the classroom.* Englewood Cliffs, NJ: Prentice-Hall.

This book contains over one hundred techniques which are designed to enhance one's sense of identity and self-esteem. The suggestions are specific, usable and have been classroom tested at all grade levels from kindergarten through college.

Chase, L. (1975). *The other side of the report card.* Santa Monica, CA: Goodyear Publishing Company Inc.

Classroom activities presented in this book center on values, attitudes, feelings of self-worth and interpersonal communication/all of which are goals of education.

Clarke, J.I. (1978). *Self-esteem: A family affair.* Minneapolis, MN: Winston Press.

Many options and good ways to deal with individual family members and family situations are discussed. Building positive self-esteem for all members through affirmation statements is taught through work sheets and exercises at the end of each chapter.

Dinkmeyer, D. & McKay, G. (1972). *Raising a responsible child.* New York: Simon and Schuster.

This book discusses practical steps to forming successful family relationships and includes an interesting analysis of the effects of our American society of the 1970s on children.

Dinkmeyer, D. & Losoncy, L. (1980). *The encouragement book: Becoming a positive person.* Englewood Cliffs, NJ: Prentice-Hall.

Whether a student needs guidance, a co-worker requires motivation, or a family member needs a boost, this book shows how to help when someone needs emotional support.

Dobson, J. (1979). *Hide or seek.* Old Tappan, NJ: Fleming H. Revell Co.

In this book Dobson exposes what he perceives to be the false value system of our society and presents ten comprehensive strategies through which parents and teachers can cultivate self-esteem in every child. In the expanded and updated edition, he further develops these issues and identifies two important new concepts: teaching children to be kind and defusing the bomb of inferiority.

Dodson, F. (1973). *How to parent.* New York: New American Library.

This book is a guide for parents of infants to preschoolers on their social, emotional and intellectual development. Its greatest contribution is in creative ways to enrich children's experiences during the pre-school years and thus stimulate their intellectual curiosity and ability.

Dreikurs, R. & Grey, L. (1968). *Logical consequences: A new approach to discipline.* New York: B.F. Dutton.

This book gives a background in child development and a rather complete theoretical explanation of logical consequences. Over half of the book is devoted to examples and discussions. Some background in psychology would be helpful in understanding this since some technical language is used.

Dreikurs, R. & Soltz, V. (1964). *Children: The challenge.* Columbia, SC: Meredith Press.

This book is written for parents. An excellent guide for parents, it gives both theory and numerous examples in layman's language.

Elkind, D. (1981). *The hurried child: Growing up too fast too soon.* Reading, MA: Addison-Wesley Publishing Co.

This book discusses the stressful effects on children of parental divorce, role conflict and job dissatisfaction. Elkind explores the burdens of today's children and offers insights, advice and hope for solving those problems.

Elkind, D. (1983). *All grown up and no place to go.* Reading, MA: Addison-Wesley Publishing Co.

Dr. Elkind feels there are two ways of growing in the U.S. today; by integration or substitution. He feels that growing up by integration helps a child resist peer pressure, have a strong concept of self, and have a strategy for managing stress which is so prevalent in our high tech society. Raising a child by integration takes dedication of time and energy by the parent to parental tasks.

Fugit, E.D. (1983). *He hit me back first: Creative visualization activities for parenting and teaching.* Rolling Hills Estates, CA: Jalmar Press.

This book provides creative activities for parents and teachers to harmoniously integrate the whole personality/-the physical, emotional, mental and spiritual aspects of one's self utilizing the will, intuition and creative imagination. For children it is a method of getting in touch with the "wise part within."

Gordon, T. (1970). *P.E.T. -Parent effectiveness training.* New York: A Plume Book Publication, New American Library.

This book is used in P.E.T. courses taught by Effectiveness Training Associates, Inc. It deals with techniques to improve communication.

Heinig, R.B. & Stillwell, L. (1974). *Creative dramatics for the classroom teacher.* Englewood Cliffs, NJ: Prentice-Hall.

This text guides teachers through a step-by-step explanation of various creative dramatic activities relying heavily on literature for ideas to dramatize. The final bibliography lists story and poetry anthologies suitable for dramatizing.

Ilg, F. & Ames, L. (1955). *Child's behavior: From birth to ten.* New York: Harper and Row.

The classic study from the Gesell Institute.

Kuczen, B. (1982). *Childhood stress/-Don't let your child be a victim.* New York: Delacorte Press.

The importance of stress management techniques for adults is well known and well publicized. This book is the first to recognize that stress management for children is equally important.

McDermott, J. (1982). *Sibling rivalry.* New York: Wideview Books.

Here is a plan for dealing with children's fights and a strategy for making them fewer and farther between.

Mercer, J. (1979). *Small people: How children develop and what you can do about it.* Chicago: Nelson-Hall.

This book presents a flexible approach to raising a child. It stresses the basic things small people do and it underscores the wide variations in development. It includes a discussion of behavior modification techniques.

Morrison, K. & Thompson, M. (1985). *Feeling good about me.* Minneapolis, MN: Education Media Corporation.

One of the most significant contributions to education in the past decade has been the introduction of "feelings" into the school curriculum. This book presents a set of prepared activities that parents, teachers and students can use to help children develop more positive and realistic self-image through exploring and learning more about themselves and the world around them. The activities center around the child's feelings.

Packard, V. (1983). *Our endangered children, growing up in a changing world.* Boston: Little Brown, and Company.

In this sweeping exploration of modern child rearing, Vance Packard argues that our institutions are seriously malfunctioning in preparing children for adulthood, and tells us what we can do to help our children. Mr. Packard states we have developed an anti-child culture with changes in the structure and setting of family life have a profound and often ill effect on children's well-being. He gives nine adult skills that help children thrive.

Satir, V. (1972). *Peoplemaking.* Palo Alto, CA: Science and Behavior Books, Inc.

Parents are in the business of "peoplemaking." This catchy, thought-provoking word is the title of a book by Virginia Satir, an expert in family therapy. Sprinkled throughout the book's chapters on how to be a more nurturing parent are experiments in communication which any reader can use with others.

Schmuck, R.A. & Schmuck, Patricia A. (1976). *Group processes in the classroom, second edition.* Dubuque, IA: Wm. C. Brown Company Publishers.

This book includes explanation about group processes and group dynamics theory as applied to the classroom, cohesiveness and sequential stages of group development.

Schuncke, G.M. & Krogh, S.L. (1983). *Helping children choose: Resources, strategies, and activities for teachers of young children.* Glenview, IL: Scott Foresman and Company.

Teaching social decision-making to young children requires structured activities that develop reasoning, perspective-taking and valuing skills. This book, using open ended stories appropriate for children kindergarten through third grade, helps children grow significantly in these areas.

Spolin, V. (1974). *Improvisation for the theater*, ninth printing. Evanston, IL: Northwestern University Press.

This handbook includes theory and foundations for teaching and directing theater, an outline for workshop exercises, and a section on children in theater and community theater. It is equally valuable for professional actors, teachers and children.

United States Department of Education. (1986). *What Works: Schools without drugs.* Washington, D.C.

Based upon information and research available, as well as on the experiences of schools that have fought and won the battle against illegal drugs, this booklet offers practical recommendations. It contains a description of a sample drug education program, a list of organizations that offer help and information and a clear, concise discussion of the legal issues schools face in dealing with drug abuse.

Waitley, D. (1983). *Seeds of greatness.* Old Tappan, NJ: Fleming H. Revell Co.

Dr. Waitley believes that a successful person is one who is working or moving toward something one wants to accomplish, especially when that brings respect and dignity as members of the human race. The importance of feelings of self worth, positive self talk, creativity and responsibility are some of the seeds of greatness discussed in this book.

Williams, L.V. (1983). *Teaching for the two-sided mind.* Englewood Cliffs, NJ: Prentice-Hall.

The author explores the application of hemispheric research to the classroom. Explanation of scientific theories and practical instructions for activities are given. Techniques which are explained include visual thinking, fantasy, multi-sensory learning, metaphor, and music among others. This well referenced book includes notes and an annotated bibliography.

Winn, M. (1981). *Children without childhood.* New York: Random House.

The importance that children play in the lives of so many parents and the ramifications of this are presented in a very readable and compelling fashion. Childhood, as a protected time for gently growing up in innocence, is being threatened according to Winn.

Essential Elements
and Correlated Subject Areas

These five charts show how this book's lessons correlate with the various "essential elements" that are mandated to be taught in the state of Texas. Essential elements correspond with key topic words of teaching goals and student learning. The charts indicate which topics are addressed through each lesson in the subject areas of theatre arts, language arts, social studies, science and health.

Theatre Arts

Essential elements:

1. Body awareness
2. Spatial perception
3. Imitative movement & sound
4. Sensory & emotional awareness
5. Pantomime
6. Imitative dialogue
7. Interpretative movement & sound
8. Original dialogue
9. Characterization
10. Improvisation
11. Situation role-play
12. Audience etiquette
13. Analyzing character behavior
14. Recognizing dramatic conflict

Lesson titles:	1	2	3	4	5	6	7	8	9	10	11	12	13	14
1.1 Making Our Rules for Creative Drama	•	•	•	•		•								
1.2 Be an Animal	•	•	•			•								
1.3 Be an Inanimate Object	•	•	•											
2.1 Concentration: I Know What You Said	•	•	•											
2.2 Sensory Awareness: Going/Candy Store	•	•		•										
2.3 Emotional Awareness: Sad, Mad, Glad	•	•	•	•					•					
2.4 Movement: Moving In Our Own Space	•	•	•	•										
2.5 Imagination: Imagine That!	•	•		•					•					
2.6 Communication: Message	•	•	•	•		•								
2.7 Cooperation: Machine Magic	•	•	•	•	•									
3.1 Characterization: Hibernating Bears	•	•	•	•					•	•				
3.2 Dialogue: Happy Times, Happy Talk	•	•	•	•				•	•	•				
3.3 Plot: Sunken Treasure	•	•		•				•	•	•				•
3.4 Theme or Idea: Giants/Creatures	•	•		•				•	•	•				
4.1 Friendship Squeeze	•	•	•	•			•		•	•				
4.2 Smile Power Makes Others Flower	•	•	•	•					•	•				
4.3 Family Celebration	•	•							•	•			•	
4.4 Favorite Childhood Experience	•	•		•	•									
4.5 Frontier Spirit	•	•							•	•			•	
4.6 Good Feelings Museum	•	•		•	•									
4.7 Director and Cast	•	•							•	•		•		
4.8 When Things Change (Loss)	•	•	•	•			•	•	•	•	•			
5.1 Body Communication	•	•	•	•										
5.2 Hot Air Balloon	•	•	•	•										
5.3 I Am A Terrific Person	•	•	•	•					•			•		
5.4 Body and Voice Messages	•	•	•	•				•	•	•			•	•
5.5 Word Messages	•	•	•	•				•	•	•	•			
5.6 Scary Dream	•	•		•				•	•	•				
5.7 Thirty-Second Vacation	•	•		•				•	•					
5.8 Tree-Top Land	•	•		•				•	•	•				
6.1 My Special Place	•	•						•	•	•				
6.2 If Pictures Could Talk	•	•						•	•					
6.3 Feelings Graph	•	•	•	•										
6.4 Spotlight	•	•							•					
6.5 Stepping Stones	•	•	•						•	•				
6.6 Tic-Tac-Toe	•	•							•	•	•		•	•
6.7 TV Commercial for a Special Person	•	•	•					•						
7.1 Family Circle	•	•						•	•	•	•	•	•	•
7.2 Storming for Ideas	•	•						•	•	•	•	•	•	
7.3 Hearts and Heroes	•			•				•	•	•	•	•		•
7.4 What Do You Do?	•	•	•					•	•	•			•	•
7.5 Speaker's Spot	•	•		•				•	•	•	•			
7.6 The Student's Role	•	•		•	•			•	•					
7.7 We Are Problem Solvers	•	•						•	•	•	•	•	•	
8.1 The Human Body Machine	•	•						•	•	•	•		•	
8.2 Clutter Bug	•	•						•	•	•	•		•	
8.3 From a Different Point of View	•	•		•				•	•	•	•			•
8.4 Garden Competition	•	•						•	•	•	•			
8.5 Guitar, Singer, Conductor	•	•	•	•				•	•		•		•	
8.6 Range of Feelings	•	•		•									•	•
8.7 Choices to Stay Healthy	•	•						•	•	•				

Creative Drama

Language Arts

Essential elements:
1 Attention on speaker
2 Non-verbal cues
3 Active listening
4 Main idea of speaker
5 Questions/information
6 Drama
7 Words, feelings, ideas expressed
8 Clear speaking
9 Personal experiences
10 Group problem-solving
11 Oral elaboration, description

Lesson titles:	1	2	3	4	5	6	7	8	9	10	11
1.1 Making Our Rules for Creative Drama	•	•	•	•	•	•	•	•			
1.2 Be an Animal	•			•	•	•	•	•			
1.3 Be an Inanimate Object	•			•	•	•	•	•			
2.1 Concentration: I Know What You Said	•			•	•	•	•	•		•	
2.2 Sensory Awareness: Going/Candy Store	•		•	•	•	•	•			•	
2.3 Emotional Awareness: Sad, Mad, Glad	•	•		•	•	•	•			•	
2.4 Movement: Moving In Our Own Space	•			•	•	•	•			•	
2.5 Imagination: Imagine That!	•				•	•	•	•		•	
2.6 Communication: Message	•				•	•	•	•		•	
2.7 Cooperation: Machine Magic	•			•	•	•	•			•	
3.1 Characterization: Hibernating Bears	•			•	•	•	•	•		•	
3.2 Dialogue: Happy Times, Happy Talk	•			•	•	•	•	•		•	
3.3 Plot: Sunken Treasure	•			•	•	•	•	•		•	
3.4 Theme or Idea: Giants/Creatures	•			•	•	•	•	•		•	
4.1 Friendship Squeeze	•	•	•				•		•	•	
4.2 Smile Power Makes Others Flower	•	•	•						•	•	•
4.3 Family Celebration	•			•	•	•	•	•	•	•	
4.4 Favorite Childhood Experience	•			•	•	•	•	•	•	•	
4.5 Frontier Spirit	•			•	•	•	•	•	•	•	
4.6 Good Feelings Museum	•			•	•	•	•	•	•	•	
4.7 Director and Cast	•			•	•	•	•	•	•	•	
4.8 When Things Change (Loss)	•	•	•	•	•	•	•	•	•	•	
5.1 Body Communication	•	•	•	•	•	•	•	•	•	•	
5.2 Hot Air Balloon	•			•	•	•	•	•	•	•	
5.3 I Am A Terrific Person	•	•	•	•	•	•	•	•	•	•	
5.4 Body and Voice Messages	•	•	•	•	•	•	•	•	•	•	
5.5 Word Messages	•	•	•	•	•	•	•	•	•	•	
5.6 Scary Dream	•		•	•	•	•	•	•	•	•	
5.7 Thirty-Second Vacation	•			•	•	•	•	•	•	•	
5.8 Tree-Top Land	•	•		•	•	•	•	•	•	•	
6.1 My Special Place				•	•		•	•	•		
6.2 If Pictures Could Talk	•	•	•		•	•	•	•	•	•	
6.3 Feelings Graph		•		•			•		•		•
6.4 Spotlight	•	•	•				•	•	•		
6.5 Stepping Stones	•		•		•		•	•			
6.6 Tic-Tac-Toe	•		•			•	•	•			
6.7 TV Commercial for a Special Person			•			•	•				•
7.1 Family Circle	•	•	•	•	•	•	•	•	•	•	
7.2 Storming for Ideas	•		•	•	•	•	•	•	•	•	•
7.3 Hearts and Heroes	•		•	•	•	•	•	•	•	•	
7.4 What Do You Do?	•		•	•	•	•	•	•	•	•	
7.5 Speaker's Spot	•		•	•	•	•	•	•	•	•	
7.6 The Student's Role	•		•	•	•	•	•	•	•	•	
7.7 We Are Problem Solvers	•		•	•	•	•	•	•	•	•	
8.1 The Human Body Machine	•			•	•	•	•	•			
8.2 Clutter Bug	•			•	•	•	•		•	•	
8.3 From a Different Point of View	•			•	•	•	•	•	•	•	
8.4 Garden Competition	•			•	•	•	•				•
8.5 Guitar, Singer, Conductor	•			•	•	•	•	•	•	•	
8.6 Range of Feelings	•		•	•	•	•	•	•	•	•	
8.7 Choices to Stay Healthy	•	•	•	•	•	•	•	•	•	•	

Social Studies

Essential elements:

Lesson titles:	1 Responsibility for self	2 Responsibility for others	3 Cooperation	4 Safety, rules, laws	5 Acceptable behavior	6 Self-awareness	7 Family composition	8 Positive traits/democratic values	9 Individual differences	10 Family needs	11 Decision-making	12 Patriotism	13 Traditions/celebrations	14 Early settlement	15 Historical leaders
1.1 Making Our Rules for Creative Drama	●	●		●	●		●				●				
1.2 Be an Animal				●		●		●							
1.3 Be an Inanimate Object				●		●		●							
2.1 Concentration: I Know What You Said	●	●	●		●	●									
2.2 Sensory Awareness: Going/Candy Store	●					●									
2.3 Emotional Awareness: Sad, Mad, Glad	●			●		●	●		●						
2.4 Movement: Moving In Our Own Space	●			●	●	●	●								
2.5 Imagination: Imagine That!				●		●									
2.6 Communication: Message	●	●		●	●		●								
2.7 Cooperation: Machine Magic	●	●		●	●	●									
3.1 Characterization: Hibernating Bears				●		●	●	●							
3.2 Dialogue: Happy Times, Happy Talk	●	●	●												
3.3 Plot: Sunken Treasure			●	●											
3.4 Theme or Idea: Giants/Creatures				●			●								
4.1 Friendship Squeeze	●	●	●	●	●	●									
4.2 Smile Power Makes Others Flower	●	●	●		●	●		●	●						
4.3 Family Celebration	●	●	●				●	●	●	●	●		●		
4.4 Favorite Childhood Experience	●						●	●		●					
4.5 Frontier Spirit	●	●	●	●	●			●				●	●	●	●
4.6 Good Feelings Museum	●	●	●	●	●	●		●							
4.7 Director and Cast	●			●	●		●	●	●						
4.8 When Things Change (Loss)	●	●		●	●		●	●		●	●				
5.1 Body Communication	●	●		●	●		●	●							
5.2 Hot Air Balloon	●	●	●		●	●									
5.3 I Am A Terrific Person	●	●	●			●		●	●						
5.4 Body and Voice Messages	●			●	●		●	●							
5.5 Word Messages	●			●		●		●							
5.6 Scary Dream	●			●		●									
5.7 Thirty-Second Vacation	●			●			●	●			●	●	●		
5.8 Tree-Top Land	●	●	●		●		●	●							
6.1 My Special Place	●				●		●	●							
6.2 If Pictures Could Talk	●	●	●		●	●		●	●		●		●		
6.3 Feelings Graph	●	●	●		●	●		●	●						
6.4 Spotlight	●	●	●		●		●	●							
6.5 Stepping Stones	●	●	●		●	●			●						
6.6 Tic-Tac-Toe	●	●	●	●		●		●	●		●				
6.7 TV Commercial for a Special Person	●	●	●	●	●			●	●						
7.1 Family Circle	●	●	●	●	●			●	●	●	●	●			
7.2 Storming for Ideas	●	●	●	●	●			●	●	●	●		●		
7.3 Hearts and Heroes	●	●	●	●	●			●	●			●	●	●	●
7.4 What Do You Do?	●	●	●	●	●			●	●		●				
7.5 Speaker's Spot	●	●	●	●	●			●	●	●	●				
7.6 The Student's Role	●	●	●	●	●			●	●	●	●				
7.7 We Are Problem Solvers	●	●	●	●	●				●	●		●			
8.1 The Human Body Machine	●	●	●	●	●				●	●		●			
8.2 Clutter Bug	●			●	●				●	●		●			
8.3 From a Different Point of View	●						●			●	●				
8.4 Garden Competition	●			●	●	●	●	●							
8.5 Guitar, Singer, Conductor	●	●	●			●									
8.6 Range of Feelings	●	●	●		●	●			●		●				
8.7 Choices to Stay Healthy	●	●	●	●		●			●	●					

Science

Health

Essential elements:
1 Daily health practice
2 Rest, sleep, exercise
3 Nutrition
4 Diseases
5 Family related health
6 Personal responsibility
7 Poisonous substances
8 Environmental hazards
9 Alcohol, drug abuse
10 Pollution
11 Care of body systems
12 Interdependence of people/env'nt
13 Environment

Lesson titles:

Lesson	1	2	3	4	5	6	7	8	9	10	11	12	13
1.1 Making Our Rules for Creative Drama						•						•	
1.2 Be an Animal												•	
1.3 Be an Inanimate Object												•	
2.1 Concentration: I Know What You Said						•		•				•	
2.2 Sensory Awareness: Going/Candy Store	•	•				•							
2.3 Emotional Awareness: Sad, Mad, Glad	•					•						•	
2.4 Movement: Moving In Our Own Space	•					•						•	
2.5 Imagination: Imagine That!												•	
2.6 Communication: Message					•	•							
2.7 Cooperation: Machine Magic						•						•	
3.1 Characterization: Hibernating Bears						•							
3.2 Dialogue: Happy Times, Happy Talk												•	
3.3 Plot: Sunken Treasure								•			•	•	
3.4 Theme or Idea: Giants/Creatures											•	•	
4.1 Friendship Squeeze								•			•	•	
4.2 Smile Power Makes Others Flower	•				•	•				•	•	•	•
4.3 Family Celebration				•	•	•						•	
4.4 Favorite Childhood Experience				•									
4.5 Frontier Spirit	•		•	•	•	•		•		•	•	•	•
4.6 Good Feelings Museum	•					•				•			
4.7 Director and Cast	•					•		•			•		
4.8 When Things Change (Loss)	•	•			•	•					•		
5.1 Body Communication						•					•		
5.2 Hot Air Balloon						•			•	•	•	•	•
5.3 I Am A Terrific Person	•					•					•		
5.4 Body and Voice Messages	•	•				•					•	•	
5.5 Word Messages	•					•					•	•	
5.6 Scary Dream	•	•				•					•		
5.7 Thirty-Second Vacation	•					•					•	•	•
5.8 Tree-Top Land	•					•		•			•	•	•
6.1 My Special Place	•	•				•					•	•	
6.2 If Pictures Could Talk	•					•					•	•	
6.3 Feelings Graph	•					•					•		
6.4 Spotlight	•					•							
6.5 Stepping Stones	•			•	•	•					•	•	
6.6 Tic-Tac-Toe	•	•		•	•	•		•			•	•	
6.7 TV Commercial for a Special Person						•							
7.1 Family Circle	•	•			•	•					•	•	
7.2 Storming for Ideas	•				•	•						•	
7.3 Hearts and Heroes	•				•	•						•	
7.4 What Do You Do?	•				•	•	•	•	•		•	•	
7.5 Speaker's Spot	•					•					•	•	
7.6 The Student's Role	•					•					•	•	
7.7 We Are Problem Solvers	•			•	•	•							
8.1 The Human Body Machine	•	•	•	•	•	•					•	•	
8.2 Clutter Bug	•			•	•	•					•		
8.3 From a Different Point of View	•		•	•	•	•		•			•	•	•
8.4 Garden Competition	•			•	•	•					•	•	•
8.5 Guitar, Singer, Conductor	•					•					•	•	
8.6 Range of Feelings	•	•		•	•	•	•	•	•		•		
8.7 Choices to Stay Healthy	•	•	•	•	•	•	•	•	•		•		

Creative Drama